Basics of Developmentally Appropriate Practice

An Introduction for Teachers of Children 3 to 6

Carol Copple and Sue Bredekamp

National Association for the Education of Young Children
Washington, DC

Cover and inside illustrations by David Clark.
Spot art: p. 13, Natalie Klein Cavanagh; p. 20, Harriet M. Johnson, used by
permission of Bank Street College of Education Publications.

National Association for the Education of Young Children
1313 L Street, NW, Suite 500, Washington, DC 20005-4101
202-232-8777 or 800-424-2460
www.naeyc.org

Through its publications program the National Association for the Education of
Young Children (NAEYC) provides a forum for discussion of major issues and
ideas in the early childhood field, with the hope of provoking thought and
promoting professional growth. The views expressed or implied are not necessarily
those of the Association.

Carol Copple, publications director. Bry Pollack, senior editor.
Malini Dominey, production and design. Natalie Cavanagh and Leah Pike, edito-
rial assistants. Patricia von Brook, copyeditor.

Library of Congress Control Number: 2005936441
ISBN-13: 978-1-928896-26-5
NAEYC Item #259

About the Authors

Carol Copple works in publications and professional development at NAEYC. She was on the faculty at Louisiana State University and the New School for Social Research. At the Educational Testing Service she codeveloped and directed a research-based model for preschool education and conducted research on children's cognition and learning. Dr. Copple joined Sue Bredekamp to edit NAEYC's 1997 volume *Developmentally Appropriate Practice in Early Childhood Programs, Rev. Ed.* She coauthored *Learning to Read and Write: Developmentally Appropriate Practices for Young Children* (NAEYC) and *Educating the Young Thinker: Classroom Strategies for Cognitive Growth* (Erlbaum) and has also written extensively for parents. She received her doctorate from Cornell University.

Sue Bredekamp is director of research at the Council for Professional Recognition in Washington, DC. She has served as a consultant for RISE Learning Solutions and for the Head Start Bureau. She developed and taught a satellite television course on early literacy, HeadsUp! Reading. From 1981 to 1998 she was director of accreditation and professional development at NAEYC. In that role she coauthored numerous influential position statements and publications of the Association, including accreditation standards, developmentally appropriate practice, curriculum and assessment, and learning to read and write. Her doctorate is from the University of Maryland.

Contents

List of Boxes

About This Book

Our purpose in this short book is to give readers a brief introduction to the basics of developmentally appropriate practice, with a focus on children ages 3, 4, and 5.

The term *developmentally appropriate practice*, or DAP for short, captures a set of core ideas that inform the work of early childhood educators. To gain a thorough understanding of DAP and use it effectively in the classroom, there is much more to learn and think about than is covered here. As the box on page ix, **Where Did DAP Come From?,** describes, we have detailed the principles and guidelines of developmentally appropriate practice more fully and for children from birth to age 8 in a larger volume (Bredekamp & Copple 1997). A number of other publications address it (e.g., Hart, Burts, & Charlesworth 1997; Gestwicki 1999; Kostelnik, Soderman, & Whiren 1999), and still others apply the principles of developmentally appropriate practice to specific areas of the curriculum, such as literacy and math (e.g., Copley 2000; Neuman, Copple, & Bredekamp 2000). As you continue to study and work in the early childhood education field, you will want to get to know that larger DAP book, as well as some of the many other DAP resources that the National Association for the Education of Young Children (NAEYC) and similar publishers have produced for teachers, caregivers, administrators, and families.

We offer this book as a first step in your becoming acquainted with the key elements of developmentally appropriate practice. If you are new to the field, it will introduce you to these core ideas that define this field you are entering. If you have been working with children for some years already, you will find much in this primer that is familiar. We hope it will give you a clearer picture of why you do some of the things you do in the classroom and why certain of them work better than others. And that you will be able to better communicate with families about what goes on in your program. Whether you are new or experienced, we hope this book will enable you to improve the effectiveness of your work with young children.

What's in this book?

This book is divided into three main parts. The first, **What Is Developmentally Appropriate Practice?,** explains what we mean by DAP and why the decisions that teachers make are so important.

Part two, **The Developmentally Appropriate Practitioner,** provides five key aspects of good teaching that enact DAP principles: creating a caring community of learners, teaching to enhance development and learning, planning appropriate curriculum, assessing children's development and learning, and developing reciprocal relationships with families. Each chapter includes examples and illustrations of developmentally appropriate practice in action.

The third part of the book, **FAQs,** answers the most common inquiries about developmentally appropriate practice we have received from educators, administrators, and parents over the years. They will help you in communicating about its realities and myths and further increase your understanding of the concept.

Finally, we have included an overview of learning and development for young children at different ages, plus references and resources to help guide you on your path to becoming a developmentally appropriate practitioner.

A quick item about vocabulary: In this book the word *teacher* is used to refer to any adult responsible for a group of children in any early childhood program, including caregivers in center-based and family child care and specialists in other disciplines who fulfill the role of teacher. Similarly, *class* and *classroom* are intended to imply not only a center setting but any grouping of young children and teachers.

Where did DAP come from?

That a given activity might be developmentally suited (or not) to children of a particular age level was hardly a novel idea when NAEYC first addressed it. Psychologists and educators had long used the concept. But the need for a more specific description became obvious in the mid-1980s, when NAEYC created a system to accredit early childhood programs. Because the accreditation guidelines required programs to provide "developmentally appropriate experiences" and materials for children, NAEYC needed to give some specifics of what that phrase meant.

Such a description was to be based on what early childhood educators knew about young children through child development theory, research, and practice. NAEYC took the lead in involving the field in considering what practices are developmentally appropriate in working with children of various ages. A position statement on developmentally appropriate practice for preschool children was published in 1986 and expanded in 1987 to cover the full birth to 8-year-old age range.

From the beginning, the description of what was developmentally appropriate was seen as dynamic rather than set in stone—nothing more or less than the best thinking of the field at a particular point in time. Any position statement on DAP would of course be revisited periodically to reflect evolution in the knowledge and thinking of the field. In 1994 the process of considering revisions to the 1987 statement got under way. For two years a panel invited input from the field at conferences and other forums, read the latest research and criticism relating to DAP, worked, talked, and debated. The results of its work were then offered to the field for more comment and refinement.

The result was a new statement on developmentally appropriate practice (NAEYC 1996). Adopted by the NAEYC Governing Board and published as part of the book *Developmentally Appropriate Practice in Early Childhood Programs* (Bredekamp & Copple 1997), the statement describes the major points of consensus in the early childhood field. Although some individuals disagree with aspects, most early childhood professionals express general agreement with the basic principles and guidelines of developmentally appropriate practice that NAEYC has articulated.

What Is Developmentally Appropriate Practice?

The Main Idea

Developmentally appropriate practice (DAP) means teaching young children in ways that

◆ **meet children where they are,** as individuals and as a group; and

◆ **help each child reach challenging and achievable goals** that contribute to his or her ongoing development and learning.

There's a little more to it than that, but that's the main idea.

For early childhood teachers, understanding how young children learn and develop is essential. The more you can know about and tune into the way the children in your class think and learn, the more effective and satisfying your work with them will be. You will gain a clearer sense of direction to guide your actions, from setting up the classroom to planning curriculum.

Meeting children where they are

Our own school-day memories are likely to be full of laboring over worksheets and tests or sitting in desks while listening to the teacher lecture. These images don't give us much help for creating good early childhood classrooms. Elsewhere in this book, you'll be reading more about how young children learn and how this varies with age and level of development. A broad picture of learning and development and what children are like at different ages, however, is not all you need in order to teach in a developmentally appropriate way. You won't meet with much success if you consider only what is "typical" of an age group, and if you try to teach children in a one-size-fits-all way. Let's step out of the early childhood setting for a moment and visit an everyday scene that illustrates both of these points.

> Coach Todd is a winning soccer coach in a league for girls ages 13–15. He has a good sense of what girls this age enjoy, what they're capable of, and what's usually tough for them, and he has experience in what works in coaching them. Bringing this general knowledge with him on the first day of practice, he knows he won't use the advanced techniques he might with college varsity players, nor will he start out too simply by explaining, "You use your foot to kick the ball." He can make some general plans based on his understanding of what is typical of this age group.
>
> Now, as this season's girls take the field for the first time, Coach Todd watches each one closely and also watches how the team plays together. He gets a feel for each player—her strengths and weaknesses, her temperament, how much experience she has. Based on all this, the coach decides where to start the girls' training, and then keeps watching and making adjustments for each individual player and the team as a whole as the season goes along.

A successful coach like Coach Todd knows he has to meet learners where they are, as individuals and as a group. Pitch the instruction too low and you not only waste learners' time but also show disrespect; pitch it too high and they feel incompetent and frustrated. This is a basic fundamental of any teaching.

Good classroom teachers continually observe children's play and their interaction with the physical environment and with other children in order to learn about each child's interests, abilities, and developmental progress. On the basis of this individualized information, along with general knowledge about the age group, we plan experiences that enhance children's learning and

Basics of Developmentally Appropriate Practice

development. With a classroom of 4-year-olds, for example, meeting learners where they are might look something like this:

> Marica notices that Tim has become fascinated with an anthill on the playground and suggests he get the magnifying glass to examine the ants and their activities more closely. A little later she checks back to find him on his stomach in the dirt, magnifying glass in hand. She decides that tomorrow she'll bring in a book on ants, maybe even help the child find a good Web site on what ants do—or both of these things.

> Because some children in her class understand only a little English, Lisa knows she will want to provide nonverbal clues to meaning wherever possible, for example, pictures, objects, gestures, and demonstrations.

> Several of the children in Ross's class never go to the computer area, and he learns their families do not have computers. He arranges opportunities to involve the children in doing simple things on the computer that relate to their favorite activities and interests, such as creating signs for their restaurant in the dramatic play area.

Helping children reach challenging and achievable goals

Meeting learners where they are is essential, but no good coach simply *leaves* his players where they are. Coach Todd's aim is always to help each girl improve her soccer skills and understanding as much as she is able, while also making sure she still enjoys the game and wants to continue playing it.

In teaching, these same principles hold. Learners will gain most from materials or experiences that build on what they already know and can do, but also make them stretch a reasonable amount toward what they don't yet know or cannot yet do.

Take the case of picking out books for 4-year-olds. The simple board books that would be fine for a toddler or even an older infant would not be challenging for most preschoolers, and chapter books would be well beyond the ability of most 4-year-olds for several more years. The preschool child is more likely to benefit from picture books that not only use many words he already knows in familiar ways but also offer a range of new vocabulary, sentence structure, and

expression that he has to work a bit to master. Because such books introduce him to new ideas and experiences, they will propel the child forward and get him ready for more advanced books. Equally important, he will find the just-within-reach books very satisfying and engrossing.

When such a fit exists—that is, when materials or experiences are challenging but not unreasonably beyond the child's ability—we say those materials or experiences are developmentally appropriate for that learner.

Developmentally appropriate practice refers to teaching decisions that vary with and adapt to the age, experience, interests, and abilities of individual children within a given age range.

✳   ✳   ✳

Here are a few generalizations, then, that can be made about developmentally appropriate teaching:

◆ Meet learners where they are, taking into account their physical, emotional, social, and cognitive development and characteristics.

◆ Identify goals for children that are both challenging and achievable—a stretch, but not an impossible leap.

◆ Recognize that what makes something challenging and achievable will vary, depending on the individual learner's development in all areas; her store of experiences, knowledge, and skills; and the context within which the learning opportunity takes place.

A cornerstone of developmentally appropriate teaching is *intentionality*. Teaching that meets learners where they are and that helps them to reach challenging and achievable goals does not happen by chance. In everything good teachers do—from setting up the classroom to assessing children to planning the curriculum—they are intentional. They are purposeful and thoughtful about the actions they take, and they base their actions on the outcomes the program is trying to help children reach. Even in responding to unexpected opportunities—"teachable moments"—the intentional teacher is guided by those outcomes.

An intentional teacher has clearly defined learning goals for children, thoughtfully chooses teaching strategies that will enable children to achieve these goals, and continually assesses children's progress and adjusts strategies to reach those goals. Having their goals and plans in mind, intentional teachers are well prepared to tell others—parents, administrators, colleagues—about what they are doing. Not only do they know what to do, they also know why they are doing it and can describe that rationale.

Deciding What Is Developmentally Appropriate

Teachers who are committed to developmentally appropriate practice enact that commitment in the decisions they make about materials, interactions, curriculum, and instruction. To make good decisions they must know a lot about the children in their classroom. Where *are* those children in their learning and development? Individually and as a group? Which goals will be challenging and achievable for them, and which would be an unreasonable stretch?

Three fundamental considerations should guide us in our information gathering and decision making:

1. Consider what is age appropriate—that is, based on what we know about the development and learning of children within a given age range.

Children are not miniature adults. They think and play and feel and see the world in ways that are different from the way that adults do,

Think about the difference between a 46-year-old and a 48-year-old. You probably couldn't tell which was which. Not so with children. Now think about the vast difference between a 1- and a 3-year-old, or between a 3- and a 5-year-old. What a difference two years make! For the young, even a month or a week typically brings big changes.

and these ways change as they develop and learn. Age is a significant predictor of a child's characteristics, abilities, and understandings. Knowing about these age-related characteristics, though only a starting point, is vital for early childhood teachers to be effective. (The charts in **A Changing Picture: Children at 3, 4, and 5,** beginning on page 69, summarize the abilities and behaviors common among young children of different ages.)

Teachers who know a lot about children's development are able to make broad predictions about what the children in an age group will be like and what will benefit them. This knowledge enables us to make some preliminary decisions and be fairly confident that our plans will be an appropriate starting point for that group. For example,

> Elena has 4- and 5-year-olds in her class, for whom she's planning an art activity. She knows that by age 4, young children's scribbles typically have given way to efforts to graphically represent objects in their environment. She begins planning a discussion about their recent trip to the park to prompt such drawings. Elena also makes a point of providing a range of art materials, because the fine motor skills of most of the younger children within her group will differ from those of the older class members.

So, age matters—it gets us started in gauging what approaches and experiences will be most effective for children in a particular age range. At the same time, good teachers recognize that each individual and group is different. Averages and norms never tell the whole story, do they? There are always significant individual differences, which brings us to the second dimension.

2. Consider what is individually appropriate—that is, attuned to each child in all of his or her individuality.

Effective teachers get to know the individual children in a group and observe them closely. From those observations we can make more specific plans and adjustments to accommodate those children's varying rates of development within and across various developmental areas. Some 4-year-olds in Elena's class, for example, can already do some things more typical of 5-year-olds, and a few of the older children aren't yet doing these things. Moreover, any one child's development will be uneven across different developmental areas.

Among the children in Elena's class, Julian is more advanced in his fine motor skills than he is socially or cognitively. Tomás has well-developed language skills but lacks certain fine motor skills such as using scissors or drawing with control.

In addition to their developmental differences, children also differ in many other respects—their likes and dislikes, personalities and learning styles, knowledge and skills based on prior experiences, and more. Responding to each child's individual needs and abilities is fundamental to developmentally appropriate practice and certainly applies to children with special learning needs as well as to more typically developing children. Good teaching can never be the same for all. It always requires us meeting each learner where he or she is and tailoring that learner's goals so they are always challenging and achievable.

As Elena makes plans to help all the children make significant progress in their language development and literacy, she has some overall strategies for the class. Beyond these, she has different plans and strategies in mind for the children who do not know any letters, the five children with only limited English vocabulary, the two who can already write their names and read some words, and so on.

3. Consider what is appropriate to the social and cultural contexts in which children live.

All of us growing up, first as members of our particular family and later as members of a broader social and cultural community, come to certain understandings about what our groups consider appropriate, valued, expected, admired. We learn this through direct teaching from our parents and other important people in our lives and through observing and modeling the behavior of those around us. Among these understandings we learn "rules" about how to show respect, how to interact with people we know well and those we have just met, how to regard time and personal space, how to dress, and countless other behaviors we perform every day. We typically learn the rules very early and very deeply, so we live by them with little conscious thought.

Culture is the socially transmitted behaviors, attitudes, and values shared by a group.

For the young children in our classrooms, what makes sense to them and what they are able to learn and respond to depend on the social and cultural contexts to which they are accustomed. Skilled teachers take such contextual factors into account, along with the children's ages and their purely individual differences, in shaping all aspects of the learning environment.

Young children rarely have had much experience in moving between cultures. Having lived their lives in the familiar confines of home and neighborhood, all children find venturing into the new world of the early childhood setting a very big change. But for those children whose language or social and cultural background differs from that predominating in the class, the situation is more drastic. Too often they find in this new place very little that is familiar and much that is scary and confusing.

It is the teacher's job to take the children's social and cultural experiences into account in planning the daily environment and learning experiences. As Loren Marulis writes about her classroom:

> [The goal] is creating an environment that says "everyone is welcome here. . . . " In my classroom, there is not one way of seeing, hearing, touching, tasting, or feeling things. We read books and have artifacts from many cultures, groups of people, lifestyles, and ways of being in the world. We do not study these books and artifacts as thematic units such as "Asian culture week." I use the books and artifacts that represent various cultures throughout my teaching. (2000)

Being responsive to social and cultural differences can be quite a challenge. Our own culture is so integral to who we are, so much a part of our daily experience of the world, that, like breathing, we may not even be aware of it. If ours is the predominant culture or if we are in a position of power, as a teacher is, it can be easy to ignore or devalue cultures different from ours. Even if we are aware of our own culture and respectful of others around us, we still can forget how much harder it is for young children to make the shifts that negotiating different social and cultural contexts requires.

Early childhood teachers have several responsibilities in this regard. First, we must take care not to make judgments about children's behavior without

Basics of Developmentally Appropriate Practice

taking the children's (and our own) social and cultural contexts into account. Let's look at an example.

Although many Europeans and Americans of European descent expect children to make eye contact with them, children from many Latin American and Asian cultures show respect by avoiding the gaze of authority figures. Susan is unfamiliar with this difference in cultural norms, and using her personal cultural lens, she interprets 5-year-old Hoinsu's lack of eye contact as a sign of disrespect, or perhaps inattention, and treats the child accordingly.

Developmentally appropriate shopping

To keep in mind the three kinds of knowledge that should inform our decisions about practice, let's take a developmentally appropriate shopping trip.

Suppose you are shopping for a dress for your 8-year-old goddaughter to wear to a school musical performance. Taking age as a starting point, you'll likely start in the "Girls 7–10" department. You figure that will be the right ballpark—the clothes fitting most girls in the 7 to 10 age range. This dimension is considering **age appropriateness** in decision making.

Now that you're in the right department, will you just pull any size 8 dress off the rack and take it to the register? No, there's more to consider. Let's say your goddaughter is petite in comparison with her peers. You've seen that she tends to look good in certain styles, and you know she hates pink. These preferences and characteristics will further direct your search. This dimension is considering **individual appropriateness** in decision making.

Finally, you take into account her peer group and family background. Although she may be looking for an outfit her favorite pop idol would wear, you know it wouldn't be appropriate for a school performance. And because you know that the cultural background of your goddaughter's family disposes them to dressing up for such occasions, you steer in that direction in making a choice. Weighing such knowledge is taking account of **social and cultural contexts**.

When a teacher's cultural blinders lead her to draw wrong conclusions, as Susan did, she is unable to provide a developmentally appropriate learning environment for the child.

Further, teachers must be able to forge the cultural bridges that young children need to thrive in the early childhood setting.

> From getting to know Kayla's parents and others in her neighborhood, Martin knows that the adults around Kayla do not typically ask a young child like her many questions that they already know the answer to—it's not in their culture. To smooth the child's transition to preschool, the teacher takes care to begin interacting with Kayla in ways she is more familiar with. Over time he will make greater use of questions.

The responsibility for learning about children's social and cultural contexts lies with the teacher. You can become more familiar with the social and cultural contexts of the children in your class in a variety of ways, including talking with families, visiting children's homes, and enlisting the help of community volunteers familiar with children's home cultures. Additional suggestions and detail are provided in various publications in the **Resources** list. (More about working with families comes in part two of this book.)

✳   ✳   ✳

To recap, when working with children, an effective teacher begins by thinking about what children of a given age and developmental level are like. This knowledge provides a general idea of the activities, routines, interactions, and curriculum that will be effective with them. But the teacher also has to look at children within the context of their family, community, culture, social group, past experience, and current circumstances, and she must consider each child as an individual. Only then can she make decisions that are developmentally appropriate—that is, age appropriate, individually appropriate, and culturally appropriate.

How Young Children Learn and Develop

Transporting the full set of teaching methods used with college students, middle schoolers, or even third-graders to the early childhood setting would be a dismal failure. But if young children learn best in certain ways, what are these? Young children learn through the following:

Relationships with responsive adults. In the very early years of life, the child's relationships with nurturing, responsive adults are indispensable for her learning (Shonkoff & Phillips 2000). The importance of relationships as the context for learning and development continues in the preschool years. Positive teacher-child relationships promote not only children's social competence and emotional development but also their academic learning (Pianta 2000).

Active, hands-on involvement. In and out of the classroom, young children learn best when they are actively involved. As they play, explore, experiment, and interact with people and objects, children are always trying to make sense of those experiences. Though abstract ideas are not totally beyond them, children under age 7 are most comfortable in the concrete world they see, smell, hear, taste, and touch.

Although hands-on learning opportunities suit preschoolers to a tee, equally important is for activities to be "mind-on," that is, to engage children's

thinking processes and encourage them to investigate, question, and ponder problems.

Meaningful experiences. We all learn best when information and concepts are meaningful to us, that is, connected to what we already know and understand. Although true for people of all ages, this fact about learning is even truer for young children. Children learn best when they can relate new knowledge to what they have already encountered, to what is already important to them. Then they can weave new threads into the fabric of their previous knowledge and experiences. For example, books about babies or new siblings are likely to be of interest to preschoolers, many of whom have younger sisters, brothers, or cousins. And children can visualize and learn about wolves by thinking about the dogs they've been around.

Constructing their understanding of the world. Young children are mentally active learners who are always "constructing" their knowledge or understanding of the world. That is, they are continually working to figure things out on their own terms. Although this is true of adult learners as well, young children have so much to try to make sense of in the world around them.

Even learning what a word refers to, which may sound straightforward, involves the child sorting out what that word does and doesn't include. As children engage in this process of construction, they often come up with ideas that are quite different from what adults *think* they have conveyed.

> Marcus, a 2-year-old, on several occasions hears his family members refer to his soft yellow ball with the word *ball* ("Ball, Marcus, here's your ball"). So Marcus learns that this particular object is *ball*. But if he is to generalize the word appropriately to other objects in the world, he has some figuring out to do. Maybe his parents are referring to the bright yellow color, and so any yellow thing is a ball? Or could it be anything you throw? Or is a ball anything of rounded shape, like the kitchen clock? Marcus may reach toward an orange, a balloon, or a round light fixture, saying "Ball!" And the idea that something oblong like a football could also be a ball may never occur to him.

Eventually, through many, many experiences with *ball*, the child will hone in on a concept that matches the same one adults mean when they use that term. But this does not occur overnight—there is construction to be done.

To illustrate how children construct their understanding of things they see and hear, authors Constance Kamii and Rheta DeVries tell a story about a young girl who believed in Santa Claus but was trying to make sense of her conflicting ideas and observations: "[S]he surprised her mother one day by asking, 'How come Santa Claus uses our wrapping paper?' She was satisfied for a few minutes by the explanation supplied by her mother, but then came up with the next question: 'Then how come Santa has the same handwriting as Daddy?'" (1980, 13).

Children keep putting the bits and pieces together, trying to relate them and make sense of them. This girl had bits of knowledge that seemed to collide. Her questions show she is struggling to fit together the various pieces of information she has in order to make sense of the situation.

As children play, they are actively constructing meaning. For this reason, observing play can be a window into their understandings and concerns. From her work with teachers who closely watch and think about children's play, educator Deborah Leong (2004) shared this observation:

> Four-year-old James sports a man's jacket and Rosa wears a fancy dress and shoulder purse. They walk around the dramatic play area opening and closing cupboards. James says, "Look here," as he opens a cupboard. Rosa leans over to look in and nods. Finally the two sit down with a piece of paper. Curious, the teacher asks, "What are you two doing?" James replies, "She's looking at the place. She's signing." Now the teacher makes the connection. The previous weekend, James and his parents had finally moved out of the shelter and into an apartment, much to his delight. Today he is playing the role of a property manager showing an apartment, and Rosa is signing a lease.

Clearly, James has been intently watching and listening to the grownups during this momentous event in his life. Now he has in mind several things that one does when finding a place to live—check it out, sign a paper. Play is a

powerful way that children work through and try to make sense of the happenings and routines in their daily lives, which they don't entirely understand but want very much to process and take control of.

What good is play?

In play, children make choices, solve problems, converse, and negotiate. They create make-believe events and practice physical, social, and cognitive skills. As they play, children are able to express and work out emotional aspects of everyday experiences and events they find disturbing. Through playing together and taking on different roles, children also grow in their ability to see something from another person's point of view and to engage in leading and following behaviors—both of which they will need to get along well as adults (Sawyers & Rogers 1988). In all these ways, play can be a milieu unsurpassed in promoting children's development and learning.

Although we think of play as the essence of freedom and spontaneity, it is also the time when children are most motivated to regulate their own behavior according to certain "musts"—restrictions about what they can say and do because the play demands it (Bodrova & Leong 2003). They know that to stay in the play, which they very much want to do, they must follow its rules. And children monitor each other pretty closely to make sure that everyone does just that ("Sammy, you're supposed to be the daddy—daddies don't bark!"). In their pretending, children take care to follow these rules, adapting their physical actions and speech as needed—walking heavily to play an elephant, talking in a high, babyish voice to portray an infant, staying in role—and in this process they become more capable of self-regulation (Vygotsky 1934/1986).

In interactive play, as compared with more structured activities, children tend to exhibit higher language levels, more innovation and problem solving, greater empathy and cooperation, and longer attention spans (Smilansky 1990). So it's not surprising that young children's engagement in high-level play is one of the best predictors of later school success (Smilansky 1990).

But not all play is high-level play, and without adult support some children will not reach this level. From expert teachers and researchers (e.g., Jones & Reynolds 1992; Davidson 1996; Bodrova & Leong 2003), much is known about how to enhance the richness and complexity of children's play.

＊   ＊   ＊

As important as it is to recognize the active construction children engage in, this does not mean they have no need for adults to convey information and instruction to them. Children certainly don't need to discover or work out *everything* for themselves—how inefficient, indeed impossible, that would be! They need adults to teach them many things. Some of these things are most efficiently taught by direct instruction; others involve a great deal of experience and construction on the child's part.

There are in fact many ways that we can promote children's learning and development. In the course of every day, teachers must draw on a wide range of teaching strategies. We look at some of those strategies later, in the chapter **Teach to Enhance Development and Learning.**

The Developmentally
Appropriate Practitioner

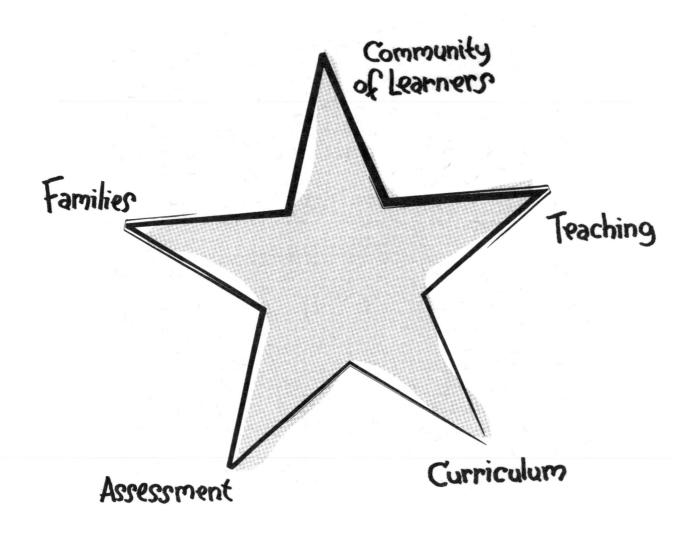

Guidelines for Developmentally Appropriate Practice

In part one we described what developmentally appropriate practice is: That it is based on knowledge of how young children develop and learn. And that it results from the process of teachers making decisions about the well-being and education of children based on what is age appropriate, individually appropriate, and appropriate to children's social and cultural contexts.

From such understanding flow guidelines to inform the practice of all early childhood teachers. That is, what teachers must *do* to enact DAP principles. Those guidelines define five key aspects of good teaching:

1. Creating a caring community of learners

2. Teaching to enhance development and learning

3. Planning appropriate curriculum

4. Assessing children's development and learning

5. Developing reciprocal relationships with families

These five aspects of teachers' work are closely interrelated. A good mental model to keep them in mind is a five-pointed star. Each point of the star represents one vital part of what teachers and early childhood programs do to achieve key goals for children. None can be left out or shortchanged without seriously weakening the whole. Now let's look at each in turn.

1. Create a Caring Community of Learners

The developmentally appropriate classroom is a place where children experience nurturing relationships, feel part of something positive, and grow into responsible members of a democratic society. Children learn and develop best when they are part of a community of learners—a community in which all participants consider and contribute to one another's well-being and learning.

To create such a classroom community, teachers

◆ get to know each child's personality, abilities, and ways of learning;

◆ make sure that all children get the support they need to develop relationships with others and feel part of the group;

◆ work to build a strong sense of group identity among the children—to develop what is sometimes called "the circle of 'we'";

◆ create an environment that is organized, orderly, and comfortable for children;

◆ plan ways for children to work and play together collaboratively;

◆ bring each child's home culture and language into the shared culture of the class; and

◆ discourage tattling, teasing, scapegoating, and other practices that undermine a sense of community and make some children feel like outsiders.

The classroom community is inclusive

In a developmentally appropriate classroom, children with special learning needs are included as full participants in the social and learning environment.

Program staff use the necessary supports and strategies to ensure that each child's individual needs are met. Researchers, teachers, and parents report that children with and without disabilities benefit in many ways from inclusive programs (Odom et al. 2002). When we work to ensure that the children with special needs are truly included in all aspects of the program, not only these children benefit but *all* the children in the group gain in understanding and acceptance of the differences among people.

In a caring community of learners, everyone feels...

I belong here.
I am safe.
I matter, and everyone else in the group matters too.
When we have problems we can work them out.
Together we can do great things.

Physical environment and schedule

In establishing the kind of environment and community in which young children can thrive, teachers give thoughtful consideration to the physical environment and schedule well before the first day and then also throughout the year.

Ensure children's health and safety. The classroom environment reflects the program's goals—at the most basic level, that children be healthy and safe. Toward this end, all program staff work together to make sure that the indoor and outdoor environments meet health and safety standards. Accessibility for children with physical disabilities is also important. (See **Resources** for some publications and Web sites that can help you address safety issues.)

Creating the "circle of 'we'"

How do children come to feel they are part of a community? Let's listen in.

Teacher on the playground: "Mike, you had a pretty hard fall! Come sit here with me. Are you OK?" To children coming over to see what's happened: "Yes, Mike had a fall. Remember when Seiko fell down last week playing with the big ball. It happens. Tony, can you bring the tissue box over? We'll stay here, Mike, until you feel better."

Teacher at circle: "Let's take a few minutes to talk together about the problem at nap time yesterday. Some of you were sleepy, and some of you wanted to get up and play. I want us all to figure out how to solve this problem. You're good at helping each other. What can we all do so nap time works better this afternoon?"

Teacher at snack: "Keisha says she likes these crackers. Do you, Jess—no? How about you, Von?" On around the table. The teacher responds to each answer; the children look from one to the other, following her lead. They become very aware of one another. Each person and each response, so important to the teacher, now becomes important to each and every one.

Vignettes adapted from Stone 2001, 31–33.

Keep classrooms lively and "explorable." Beyond being a safe place, the developmentally appropriate environment continually invites children's initiative and active exploration of materials. Materials are well organized and physically within reach to enable children to readily find and use them. Effective teachers create a rich learning environment that changes often enough to be fresh and interesting to children and yet remains consistent enough to be predictable and understandable to them. Young children need to know what's available and where. But they lose interest when they find all the same materials in the classroom day after day.

Take into account evolving learning needs. Children's interests and learning needs also evolve over the course of the year. By spring they are ready

Basics of Developmentally Appropriate Practice

for greater complexity and challenge than they were on first entering the program in the fall. With an eye to keeping things interesting for children and helping them move forward in all areas, teachers change materials from day to day and over the weeks and months. Over time, for example, they might put out puzzles with more pieces, which are more challenging to solve. To help children learn the words that correspond to objects, teachers might start out by labeling the bins in which materials are kept with only pictures of the contents, next use print and pictures together, and finally use only print labels. At the water table, they might introduce new problems and stimulate new investigations by replacing children's usual materials with items that leak, such as colanders, funnels, and eyedroppers.

Carefully plan daily routines. Hand in hand with an organized physical environment is a well-thought-out daily routine. Young children like to have a sense of what will happen and when, and a consistent schedule helps them develop their sense of time and sequence. The schedule needs to be fairly predictable, but not rigid. Teachers plan for balance in the children's day: times for rest and times for vigorous activity; time outdoors as well as indoors; times to do things together in large and small groups and times to work independently (more in a later chapter on effectively using different learning contexts such as large and small groups).

Guidance in a caring community

How we interact with children shapes how they approach others, how they feel about themselves, and how they develop and learn. Our expectations for their behavior affect them too. If we expect them to behave badly, they generally will. If we expect them to make good choices and treat others respectfully, more often than not they will do that.

Guiding young children's behavior begins with building a warm, positive relationship with them. Also crucial is organizing the environment and schedule so children can do their best (e.g., not rushing an activity, not introducing new challenges at the end of the day when children can be tired and cranky),

Self-regulation is the ability to focus attention and manage one's emotions and behaviors according to the demands of the situation. The self-regulatory abilities that children gradually develop—or fail to develop—powerfully affect their interaction with people around them and influence their learning and school success.

and making learning experiences engaging and appropriate for them (e.g., so they won't be bored or unduly frustrated).

Finally, good teachers use every opportunity—and make opportunities, as well—to teach children social skills and self-regulation. In the early childhood years, guidance isn't something we do so we "can get on with the curriculum." Instead, positive social and emotional development are themselves key curricular goals for children.

Developmentally appropriate guidance shows respect for children. It helps them understand and grow, rather than punishing or shaming them. It is directed toward helping children develop self-regulation and the ability to make better decisions in the future. Teachers are using effective guidance when they

- ◆ value mistakes as learning opportunities;
- ◆ listen when children talk about their feelings and frustrations;
- ◆ guide children to resolve conflicts, and model for children the skills they need to solve problems on their own; and
- ◆ patiently remind children of rules and the rationales behind them.

When teachers work to give children a solid foundation in their emotional development and ability to relate well to others, children carry that foundation with them into their future lives in and out of school.

Basics of Developmentally Appropriate Practice

2. Teach to Enhance Development and Learning

Whatever early childhood setting you work in, you are responsible for actively supporting children's development and learning. There is no magic formula for doing this. Good teachers continually use their knowledge and judgment to make decisions about the materials, interactions, and learning experiences likely to be most effective for the group and each individual in it.

Sometimes debates on classroom practice can get cast as "either/or" choices. For example, one side shouts, "It's about phonics!" and the other declares, "No, it's whole language!" Or one camp proclaims, "Direct instruction is the way!" and the other retorts, "Only child-initiated learning works!" But if we all step back a bit, we can usually see that *both* approaches have some value and a place in the classroom—it is a matter of "both/and" rather than "either/or." So it is with teaching strategies.

Using a wide range of teaching strategies— the teacher's tool belt

Research supports the value of using multiple teaching strategies. For example, after carefully reviewing the research on effective early childhood teaching, the

National Academy of Sciences Committee on Early Childhood Pedagogy summed it up this way:

> How should teaching be done in preschool? Research indicates that many teaching strategies can work. Good teachers acknowledge and encourage children's efforts, model and demonstrate, create challenges and support children in extending their capabilities, and provide specific directions or instruction. All of these teaching strategies can be used in the context of play and structured activities. Effective teachers also organize the classroom environment and plan ways to pursue educational goals for each child as opportunities arise in child-initiated activities and in activities planned and initiated by the teacher. (Bowman, Donovan, & Burns 2000, 8)

As we think about multiple teaching strategies, consider as an analogy the constructing of a table or repairing of a roof. No skilled carpenter tries to do every part of his work with the same tool. He doesn't use a screwdriver to drive a nail into a board or a hammer to twist in a screw. Like a competent carpenter, a good teacher has many tools, or teaching strategies, in her tool belt. The teacher selects the best strategy to use at any given moment, depending on the learning goal, specific situation, and needs of the child. That is, the teacher is choosing the strategy she thinks will be most useful in the particular situation. Often she may try one strategy, see that it doesn't work, and try something else. What's important is to have a variety of strategies at the ready and to remain flexible and observant.

Below are descriptions of teaching strategies that are key to the effective teacher's repertoire. Certainly others exist, and there are many variations. Moreover, strategies often are used in combination; in a single sentence, for example, a teacher might both acknowledge a child's actions and give her a cue or challenge ("Marlena, you found the rug was 16 footsteps long; do you think it will be 16 if I walk it with my footsteps?"). We should also point out that the terms for the strategies we use below are not universal. Various education models and programs have their own special labels for what teachers do. Our purpose is simply to look at several major kinds of strategies (see Bowman, Donovan, & Burns 2000) that teachers need to have at their disposal to do their job well:

Acknowledge: give positive attention that tells the child you noticed what he said or did (*"You wrote your name on your picture"; "Thanks for your help, Mateo"*).

Encourage: offer comments or nonverbal actions that promote the child's persistence and effort (*"This is a hard one, but you all are coming up with lots of ideas"; "Ben's story tells us just what the dog looks like—I can really picture him"*), rather than giving the child evaluative praise (*"Good job, Ben"*).

Give specific feedback: offer specific rather than general comment on the child's performance (*"That's a* d, *Lily, not a* b—*it looks a lot like a* b *but it's turned the other way, see?"*).

Model: display for children a skill or desirable way of behaving (*whispering when you want the children to lower their own voices; modeling cooperation and problem solving by saying, "You both want the shovel, so let's search together for something else that would work in the sand"*).

Demonstrate: show the correct way to perform a procedure that needs to be done in a certain way (*e.g., how to use a hammer or wash one's hands thoroughly*).

Create or add challenge: generate a problem or add difficulty to a task or step so that it is a bit beyond what children have already mastered (*e.g., when the children are easily able to throw bean bags through a large hole in a box, rotating the box to offer a smaller hole; instead of having children just observe the outcome of mixing two substances, ask them to predict—"What do you think will happen when . . . ?"*).

Give a cue, hint, or other assistance: help children to work "on the edge" of their current competence (*e.g., initially labeling cubbies with both picture and print labels [the pictures to be removed later]; helping two quarreling children through the steps of conflict resolution until they can work through conflict on their own*).

Provide information: directly give children facts (*"Birds make nests like this one to live in"*), verbal labels (*"This is a cylinder"*), and other information.

Give directions: provide specific instructions for children's action or behavior *("Move the mouse to this icon and click on it"; "Pour very slowly so we don't lose any of the liquid").*

With some of these strategies, children receive new information or directions, and in others they are spurred to think and solve problems. Some strategies give children feedback to improve, some simply encourage them to persist in tackling a problem or working on a skill they haven't yet mastered. Teaching strategies differ in their uses and the demands they place on the child, but all can be valid and useful, depending on the goal and situation.

In this example, the teacher has her tool kit ready, and makes use of various strategies as needed:

> Jane teaches 3- and 4-year-olds in a Head Start center. Early in the school year, she observes that although the children like to play in the house area, they do little more than pile the dishes on the table, dump them in the sink, or open and close cupboards. Their play lacks focus and conversation, and it often breaks down into arguments. She wants to introduce the children to other possibilities and help them to play at a higher level.
>
> One day, when Ashley, Elizabeth, and Josue are in the house area, Jane joins their play. Choosing a theme that she knows these three children have experienced—birthdays—she enters the area and **models** the role of the birthday person. "Hi, I'm planning to have a party for my birthday. I wondered if you could help me?"
>
> The children quickly become interested and gather around. Jane sits at the table. "What will we need for my party?" she asks to prompt their language interaction. "A cake!" "Balloons!" "Presents!" they reply.
>
> "Whom shall we invite?" she asks. The children start shouting out names, and Jane says, "I can't remember all those names. We need to make a list." She **creates a challenge**—one she knows will vary with the individual child—by asking, "Who can write their name on the list?"
>
> Paper for the list is found, and the children begin to take turns "writing" their name or the name of a friend. For Elizabeth, Jane **gives assistance** in the form of name cards the child can copy. For Ashley, she **demonstrates** how to make the first letter of her name. For Josue, who can write at least some letters of his name on his own, she **adds more challenge.** "What comes after your *J* ?" she asks Josue. "What letter do you think your friend

Basics of Developmentally Appropriate Practice

Dariska's name starts with?" As the children write, Jane **acknowledges** and **encourages** their efforts. "You made an *N*," she tells Josue. "I know you've been practicing writing that letter every day."

When the list is made, Jane adds some mathematics to the learning experience.

"We have a long list of people to invite, but I don't know if we have enough dishes for all these people. How can we find out?" The children begin to count the people on their list and the plates in the cupboard. Sometimes a child gets stuck, at a loss for the next number. Jane supplies the appropriate counting word or several, as needed—that is, she **provides information.**

This vignette illustrates how the full range of teaching strategies may be used in any context. Although play is an open-ended activity, the teacher may directly provide information or create challenges in the play setting. Likewise in a planned small or large group, the teacher may ask questions and use other techniques to engage the children in problem solving or generating ideas.

Scaffolding children's learning

In the first chapter we saw that developmentally appropriate goals are both challenging and achievable. The most effective learning experiences build on what children already know and can do, but also make them stretch a reasonable amount toward what the children don't yet know or cannot yet do. But learners cannot spend all their time stretched "on their tiptoes." They also need plenty of opportunity to practice the skills they are in the process of acquiring. They need to feel solid mastery and a sense of being successful, of the goal having been achieved, not just rushed on to the next challenge. Once children have mastered a skill or concept, they are ready for the next stretch.

Then, as a child begins a new challenge, he may need some support from the teacher to enable him to manage it. At the same time, a skilled teacher doesn't overdo the help. The aim is to provide the least amount of support that the child needs to do something he cannot quite do on his own. For example, if the goal is to walk a balance beam, a good teacher might stand beside the child as he walks the beam, so that he can put his hand on the teacher's arm as needed to keep from falling. If, instead, the teacher held the boy's hand throughout, he would be less likely to learn to balance on his own.

As the child begins to master the new skill or acquire the new understanding, the teacher gradually reduces the support provided. Soon the child who has been receiving assistance will be able to handle the skill or task without support. Because the teacher provides the support only as long as it is needed, providing support in this way is called *scaffolding*—like the temporary structures that builders or painters stand on to get to spots high up on a house they couldn't otherwise reach.

Teachers use scaffolding to help children make progress in all areas of learning and development throughout the day. The scaffolding can take many forms, using any of the strategies listed on pages 33–34. For example, the teacher could

◆ ask a question or give another sort of hint to alert the child to some aspect of the task that has been missed (e.g., "Are you going to keep the big and little spoons together, or put them in separate piles?");

◆ add cues in a different form (e.g., provide a picture or diagram along with text to help children read a message);

◆ pair the child with another child who has complementary strengths— they will be able to do things together that neither initially could do alone; or

◆ use software that gears the cues and prompts to the individual child's needs (depending on his performance) and thus allows children to be as independent as possible and yet as "assisted" as needed.

Using a variety of learning formats

Besides being intentional about the strategies they use, the support they provide, or other teaching interactions, effective teachers think carefully about the learning context or format that is best for helping children achieve a desired outcome. The four major kinds of learning formats are large groups, small groups, play/learning centers, and routines. Each has its own characteristics, functions, and value.

Large groups. Sometimes referred to as whole group, group meeting, or circle time, the large group is ideal for class discussions, making plans, and providing children with information and experiences the teacher wants to make sure *all* the children share. Ideas may be introduced or investigations launched in the large group and followed up in small groups. The large-group setting also offers opportunities for children to learn and practice skills such as talking to the group about their experiences, listening to their classmates, responding appropriately with questions or comments, working cooperatively, and using and processing new information.

There is no hard-and-fast rule as to the recommended duration of large-group meetings. To be part of a large group and to focus attention for periods of time are themselves learning goals that young children must practice. Keeping them in large groups only briefly early in the year is wise, then lengthening the duration as the year progresses. The most important principle is to read the children's cues and not keep going after they start to lose interest. If the children are getting restless, move to a lively ending to finish on a high note.

Small groups. Working with children in small groups greatly expands the teacher's opportunities to observe them and involve each child actively. Teachers often use this format for more focused experiences, perhaps introducing a new skill or concept or engaging children in working on a problem or applying a concept already introduced. Small groups may take place during the part of the day devoted to learning centers or at a separate period of the day.

Small groups vary in size, usually ranging from three to five children. The groups may be formed on the basis of a common interest or need or may simply be several children the teacher thinks would work well together. In a small-group setting, the teacher can give children more focused attention and provide support and challenges tailored to their individual levels. He can give clues, ask follow-up questions, and notice what every child is able to do and where each has difficulty. Giving children the opportunity to engage in conversations with peers and solve problems collaboratively is yet another major plus of small-group time.

Finding ways to work with children in small groups is sometimes a challenge with a large class of children. The box **Small-Group Learning Experiences in the Real World?** on page 40 offers some ideas.

Play and engagement in learning centers. At the preschool and kindergarten levels, part of the classroom is typically divided into learning centers, or interest areas that offer children a range of options for engagement. Commonly found centers include blocks, dramatic play, library, art, and discovery/science; a teacher may also opt to use interest areas such as computers, writing, music and movement, and cooking. The play that takes place in these centers such as blocks and dramatic play is vital to children's learning and development (see **What Good Is Play?** on page 20). For each center, the teacher carefully selects materials and activities to support educational goals. She also makes a point of observing what children are doing in each center, in order to guide later planning.

An effective teacher also interacts with children frequently and purposefully during play and other center activities. She engages children in conversation, gives information or feedback, and models for children things they might do or say—using a new method with clay or paint in the art center, for example, or wondering, "Let's see, what on this menu looks good today?" in dramatic play.

Daily routines. Much valuable learning also occurs throughout the day in routines such as arrival, departure, room cleanup, hand washing, meals and snacks, and transitions. For example, in ending circle time, the teacher might have the children join in a song that plays with and highlights the phonological features of language, such as rhyme, that they need to be familiar with in order to read. At snack time they might examine a message the teacher gives them in order to see how many crackers each child gets.

Skills practiced and applied during daily routines are often practical and functional, and thus especially meaningful for children. Mealtime and snack time and other routines are times when children talk to one another, and teachers have excellent opportunities to engage children in extended conversation.

Small-group learning experiences in the real world?
Four ideas that work

A typical teaching team is a lead teacher and an assistant teacher—with at least 16 children to think about. So how can you manage to carry on focused learning experiences with small groups or work with individual children? Here are just four ways to go about it. Creative teaching teams will be able to think of more.

1. Plan a focused learning experience that children come to in groups during choice or free playtime.

Fairly common in early childhood classrooms is for teachers to plan a particular learning experience for the children to visit during their choice time. To increase the value of these experiences, teachers need to give careful thought to the focus of each activity and to creating experiences that challenge the children. Children can come to the small group as space permits (for instance, no more than four at a time). Or a teacher may invite some children herself because she thinks they would benefit from the experience and might not seek it out on their own.

2. Divide the group to make small-group learning experiences more feasible.

One adult takes half the children to the music room or the playground, while the other adult stays with the other children—eight, let's say—in the classroom. In the classroom, while four of the eight build in the block area or draw in the art area, the teacher works with the others in a focused experience for about 15 minutes. Then the two groups switch, and the teacher works with the first four children.

3. Get extra value from having classroom volunteers.

An extra adult in the classroom makes a big difference. In some programs, family members, students, or others come in regularly to read with the preschoolers or help out in other ways. The presence of another adult gives teachers more freedom to do small-group learning experiences.

4. Use various times in the children's day for small groups and other learning experiences.

During breakfast or lunch, perhaps several times a week, put place cards for four children at a special table with the teacher—sitting at the "Teacher's Table" becomes an eagerly anticipated privilege. Besides talking pleasantly with the children, the teacher may incorporate a learning experience—perhaps an idea relating to pattern or quantity, or observation and discussion of what happens when the juice is poured from a tall, thin pitcher to a short, fat one.

Adapted from U.S. Department of Health and Human Services 2003, 22.

3. Plan Appropriate Curriculum

The curriculum consists of the knowledge and skills to be taught in the educational program and the plans for experiences through which learning will take place. Vital for every early childhood program is having a curriculum in written form, and actually using it to guide planning. The curriculum guides teachers in developing and carrying out learning experiences that are consistent with the program's goals for children and connect within an organized framework. Research clearly demonstrates that children learn more in programs where there is a well-planned and implemented curriculum (Schweinhart & Weikart 1997; Bowman, Donovan, & Burns 2000; Landry 2005).

Key learning outcomes for children

Curriculum development and planning begin with the question, What should children who come out of the program know and be able to do? For a specific set of children, the teacher asks, What goals or outcomes do I want these children to achieve during the time that I am teaching them?

Good programs have always recognized that children's early physical, social, emotional, and cognitive development affects their future success and well-being, and have actively sought to promote development and learning in all these areas. Over the years the research base has grown, and now we are able to define more specifically which outcomes enable children to succeed in school and beyond.

As vital as ever is fostering children's curiosity, self-regulation, social competence, and sense of their own capacity to learn and achieve. Developing social and emotional skills—such as the ability to make friends or to regulate one's feelings and reactions—has proven important to how children fare in school and in their personal relationships. Among the areas where we need to place greater emphasis than in the past, however, are vocabulary and language proficiency, literacy knowledge and skills (e.g., phonemic awareness, alphabet knowledge, and concepts of print), and key mathematics and science concepts.

In recent years professional organizations, states, and other entities have been placing greater emphasis on defining and evaluating key learning outcomes for school-age children. This trend has now reached early childhood programs, with most states as well as Head Start programs articulating specific learning outcomes for children to achieve by the end of preschool. The following are just a few examples:

In language and literacy:

◆ Predicts what will happen next in a story (Colorado)

◆ Identifies words that rhyme (Ohio)

In mathematics:

◆ Determines "how many" in sets of five or fewer objects (South Carolina)

◆ Matches and sorts shapes (Washington State)

In social-emotional development:

◆ Shows increasing abilities to use compromise and discussion in working, playing, and resolving conflicts with peers (Head Start Child Outcomes Framework)

Making curriculum effective

As part of its standards for accreditation of early childhood programs nation-wide, NAEYC (2005b) has identified as essential the curriculum areas listed below. All these areas are important for children's learning and well-being. With minor differences here and there, this list is representative of the curriculum areas defined by many professional groups and states:

◆ social-emotional development,

◆ language development,

◆ literacy development,

◆ mathematics,

◆ technology, scientific inquiry and knowledge,

◆ understanding ourselves and our communities,

◆ creative expression and appreciation for the arts, and

◆ physical development and skills.

A good curriculum is much more than a collection of activities. It is based on the key outcomes for children, and it should provide teachers with a useful framework for choosing learning experiences and materials and for seeing how those fit together to accomplish the outcomes.

However a program arrives at its curriculum, the curriculum should be a written one and both effective and comprehensive—that is, addressing all areas of children's development and learning. Published, commercially available curriculum products, if they are consistent with the recommendations of the profession (e.g., see NAEYC & NAECS/SDE 2003) and with the program's goals, may be worth considering for use. Or, if program staff themselves have the interest, expertise, and resources to develop a curriculum, the program may decide to take that route.

Published curriculum products often focus on a specific area, such as literacy or math. These products can be useful. A program might find it valuable to use a single-subject curriculum resource in literacy, math, social studies, or another area, perhaps because the domain is one in which teachers feel they particularly want guidance and tools. But again, administrators and teachers

Adapt, articulate, advocate

What if you're not in a position to make the decision about what curriculum will be adopted for the program? As a classroom teacher or teaching assistant, this choice may not be in your hands. But even if this is the case, you are likely to have a role in selecting from choices the curriculum offers and adapting the learning experiences it offers. When you are able to articulate clearly how your adaptations will contribute to the curriculum's goals, you are more likely to be given the flexibility to make those changes.

Another possibility is that you are working in a program that either doesn't have a written curriculum or has one in name only—a curriculum book or kit, perhaps, gathering dust on the shelf rather than serving as the mainspring for teacher planning. When teachers encounter this situation, it's vital they be proactive in designing or choosing a clear curriculum plan for their group and making sure it gets used.

should not forget that the curriculum needs to be comprehensive. A single-subject curriculum resource is only a part of the picture; it should not be allowed to crowd out other learning domains. That is, no one subject area "tail" should end up wagging the whole curriculum "dog."

In addition to making sure the curriculum is comprehensive, teachers should do the following:

Use the curriculum framework in planning to give coherence to the classroom experiences.

Too often early childhood programs provide only scattered tidbits in math, science, literacy, and other domains. It's a little here, a little there, whatever happens to come up. As valuable as it is to use spontaneous opportunities in teaching, we must not leave content and sequence to chance. We must be familiar with the key content and skills in each domain (the **Resources** section

Basics of Developmentally Appropriate Practice

lists sources of guidance for each domain). Then, we must do careful planning and follow-through, carefully shaping and adapting the experiences we provide to enable each child to acquire these concepts and skills.

Consider the developmental paths that children follow in determining the sequence and pace of learning experiences.

Teachers continually consider materials and activities with an eye to moving children forward in all areas. Among the concepts and skills we want children to acquire, some things logically come first and other things build on them. For example, children need a basic understanding of counting objects before they are ready to add two groups together and determine how many are in the combined group.

We also want to select materials with individual children's interests and developmental progress in mind. Here's an example.

> Kindergarten teacher Denise notices that day after day 5-year-old James is stringing beads in an alternating *abab* pattern—red, green, red, green. Thinking he may be ready to try some new possibilities, she decides to see what happens when she sets out a few strings with other simple patterns, such as *aabb.* Knowing that pattern awareness supports mathematical understanding, Denise wants to help James to progress toward the outcome of recognizing, duplicating, and extending simple patterns.

Make meaningful connections a priority in curriculum planning.

Connected, integrated curriculum is more effective than curriculum content taught in small, unrelated chunks. We need to remember too that learning something new is easier when it builds on something we already know. Young children in particular learn best when the concepts, vocabulary, and skills they encounter are related to something they know and care about, and when the new learnings are themselves interconnected in meaningful, coherent ways.

There are several common approaches to making children's learning integrated and meaningful. When teachers use themes or projects, for instance, they can help children see how concepts and skills are related and how these matter—i.e, they are useful to us in things we want to accomplish. For instance, the child sees that counting, making a list or chart, and concepts of heat are useful in cooking or in investigating the properties of water.

In shaping projects or themes, a teacher can draw on children's own interests and also can introduce them to things he knows are likely to interest young children. Developing and extending children's interests is particularly important during the preschool years, when children's ability to focus their attention is in its early stages (Bowman, Donovan, & Burns 2000).

Depth is important too. Young children become more engaged and learn better when the curriculum is not skimming lightly over a great many areas but instead allows for sustained time with a more select set. When learning is meaningful, integrated, and in-depth, it is also more likely to stick.

4. Assess Children's Development and Learning

Curriculum is the plan for enabling children to reach desired outcomes; assessment is the process of looking at children's progress toward those outcomes.

Thoughtful attention to assessment is essential to developmentally appropriate practice. Assessing children, which includes observing them and closely considering their work, is key for teachers in their efforts to get to know each child and his or her abilities and needs. Thus, it is a vital part of "meeting learners where they are." On an ongoing basis, a teacher needs to assess each child to determine whether he or she is making expected progress toward important outcomes and to inform the planning the teacher does to promote that child's learning and development.

In developmentally appropriate programs we assess in order to

◆ monitor children's development and learning,

◆ guide our planning and decision making,

◆ identify children who might benefit from special services or supports, and

◆ report and communicate with others. (McAfee, Leong, & Bodrova 2004)

Assessment of young children's learning and progress is vital, but it requires certain understandings. In their early years, children grow and change rapidly. Their development is uneven, full of spurts and plateaus. And they can be easily distracted when you are trying to assess them. They usually are not highly motivated in formal assessment situations, to say the least. As assessment expert Tynette Hills (1992, 46) points out, young children "have limited interest in being assessed—an adult's agenda—especially when the assessment procedures interfere with their normal range of movement, talk, and expression of feelings."

Knowing these things about young children leads us to approach assessment in certain ways—and to avoid other ways—as we seek to get valid information about them. One principle is to never rely on a single measure. Information should be gathered from various sources, at various times, and in different settings or contexts. For example, because purely verbal procedures tend to underestimate children's knowledge and cognitive skills, especially for English-language learners, assessment approaches should include both verbal and nonverbal procedures (NAEYC 2005a).

Gathering assessment evidence from observing in realistic situations is also key. Such observations are more likely to reflect what children do on an everyday basis and reveal the full extent of what they are capable of doing and understanding. To round out this picture, observations should occur across different settings, such as in the classroom, on the playground, and during interactions with peers, familiar adults, and strangers. Assessments should also occur in activities across all the domains of the curriculum. If children are assessed across the curriculum in areas as diverse as art, music, and block building, there is maximal opportunity for them to demonstrate what they know and can do in ways beyond the boundaries of language (NAEYC 1995, 2005a).

Finally, as we have seen in other areas of teacher decision making, assessing children in developmentally appropriate ways requires attention to what is

◆ age-appropriate—anticipating the characteristics of children within an age range that are likely to influence the validity of our assessment methods;

- individually appropriate—which includes choosing and adapting our means of assessment to get the best information about a particular child; and

- culturally appropriate—for example, considering what will make sense to the child, given her linguistic and cultural background (e.g., avoiding

Using assessment information effectively

As teachers we don't gather information about children just to let it sit on the shelf. And those observation notes you make on little scraps? Don't leave them stuffed in your pockets. *Use* the information as you plan and teach. Experts (Jablon, Dombro, & Dichtelmiller 1999; McAfee, Leong, & Bodrova 2004) on how to make good use of assessment information offer suggestions such as these:

Plan on a daily, weekly, and long-term basis in order to provide what children need to learn and thrive.

Some teachers write out their plans in detail; others do their planning in broader strokes, adding notes relating to specific activities and individual children. Whatever method you choose, you will need to reflect and plan thoughtfully for the group as a whole and for each individual child.

Consider all relevant assessment information as you plan.

Refer to your observation notes, the information you have gathered from families, and children's work samples, as well as checklists, summary sheets, and any more formal assessment information you have available.

Use assessment information to individualize for children.

Observing how children use the environment and what they gravitate toward will help you in determining how to adapt the environment, materials, or daily routines to be responsive to individual children's interests, needs, and strengths.

For example, in recording how and when children are using different areas—let's say, who looks at books during quiet reading and choice times—you might notice that a particular child, Michael, has no tally marks next to his name. An active block builder and painter, he never goes and gets engaged with a book. You would then give some thought to what

Basics of Developmentally Appropriate Practice

materials that will not be understood), as well as interpreting her behaviors in light of the social and cultural contexts in which she lives (e.g., not taking a child's limited verbal response to the test situation to mean she is deficient in language or intellect).

Michael's special interests are and bring in some books on a favorite topic (lizards, soccer, or whatever it may be). You might read some of these with him to get him interested, either on his own or in a small group. Then observe for a few weeks to see whether his visits to the book areas increase.

Or suppose you are helping children to understand and express how objects are located in relation to each other. For the children who don't yet know *in*, *out*, *next to*, and other basic location words, plan various opportunities through which they can learn these. As for children who already have mastered the more basic concepts and vocabulary, make plans to introduce them to additional vocabulary and higher-level concepts.

Don't try to go it alone.

Look to professional organizations, such as NAEYC, International Reading Association, and National Council of Teachers of Mathematics, for guidance on assessment, curriculum, and teaching in specific content areas and for information about children's development and learning (see the **Resources** section for some suggestions). Other sources are commercial curriculum guides and the curriculum guidance produced by states, school districts, or programs.

Consider modifications to the learning environment.

Time, space, materials, learning contexts, and adult roles can all be modified to help meet children's assessed needs. For example, almost any activity you do with children can be made simpler or more complex, according to what individual children are ready for.

Make follow-up plans.

Children generally need repeated experiences with an idea or skill to get a solid grasp of the ideas, but not so often that it becomes old. Follow through to ensure children really master the skill or concept. Give careful thought to where the child or group of children might go next.

5. Develop Reciprocal Relationships with Families

Making developmentally appropriate decisions for the children in a class means knowing them as individuals. And the younger the children, the more a teacher needs to acquire much of this knowledge through relationships with their families. Asking families about their children is an extremely valuable strategy for a teacher, but that's not all. It also conveys to parents that she values their knowledge and insights.

A good teacher never displays a condescending attitude—that *she's* the one with all the information and best equipped to make all the decisions, and that parents are basically uninformed folks badly needing her wisdom and unable to make good choices for their children. On the contrary, parents are the most important people in their children's lives. They know their child well, and their preferences and choices matter. The relationship we want to create is a two-way street, with communication and respect in both directions—that is, a reciprocal relationship.

Besides drawing on families' in-depth knowledge of their children as individuals, effective teachers will also learn from families about their home and community environment, including its cultural dimensions. This knowledge is

> Reciprocal relationships require mutual respect, cooperation, shared responsibility, and negotiation of differences toward shared goals.

Basics of Developmentally Appropriate Practice

critical in making classroom decisions that are appropriate for children, as well as in fostering positive relationships with the parents themselves.

The other side of the reciprocal relationship is this: Early childhood teachers have a lot to share with families. We have valuable knowledge and experience of children in general. And we can give parents the particulars about what their own child said and did that day, what he is exploring, learning, and achieving in the class. Family members greatly value this information and love to hear about these moments in their young child's life. In addition, when they

---

Creating two-way relationships with families

Here are some basic tips for building solid, reciprocal relationships with parents:

◆ Make parents welcome in the classroom, and invite their participation in the program and in decision making for their child's care and education.

◆ Don't come on as the all-knowing professional who has all the answers. Instead, try to create a relationship that allows for open dialogue.

◆ Maintain frequent, positive, two-way communication with families. Planned conferences and messages or letters sent home to parents are important, as is day-to-day communication with families. You want parents to feel comfortable sharing their knowledge and concerns about their child. And you want to make sure they know about the good things that are going on with their child every day, not just about problems that arise. Then anytime you do have a concern or question, you can raise it without the parents feeling threatened.

◆ Acknowledge parents' choices and goals for their children and respond with sensitivity and respect to their preferences and concerns. This doesn't mean you should defer to parents even when you think their desire isn't good for the child. You have a professional responsibility to the children, first and foremost. But in a difference of opinion about what's best, keep in mind that your goal is not to win—this would mean the parents would *lose*! Rather, the goal is to come to a meeting of the minds in which both parties listen to each other's concerns and views and together search for a solution that addresses shared goals for the child.

Basics of Developmentally Appropriate Practice

learn about the child's school life, they are better able to talk with him about his experiences and build on these experiences at home.

Teacher-parent communication is important too in achieving a degree of consistency in the ways that the significant adults in the child's life guide and relate to that child. There isn't likely to be much consistency without communication. Still another plus is that children feel more secure when they see that the adults who care about them—their parents and teachers, in this case—are themselves in a positive relationship and share trust and respect.

When it comes to making decisions about a child, sharing that decision making with families is important. For example,

> Will's parents are upset that he doesn't bring home worksheets, and they argue that his teacher should start using workbooks in class. But from her knowledge of the research and her classroom experience, Glenda knows that worksheet learning is not very effective with preschool children.
>
> Glenda could just insist that she is right and the parents are wrong. But instead, she takes a step back and asks these parents about their goals for their child. They are very concerned that Will won't be ready to enter and succeed in school. Because the child's school success is one of Glenda's goals too, she can tell Will's parents about the strategies she is using to help Will learn in key areas. She gives further thought to what she could share with the parents to show Will's progress.

Making "common cause" around a goal is a good starting point for a partnership with a family. This conversation also prompts Glenda to consider whether she could do more in terms of displaying and sending home work samples and other visible evidence (other than worksheets) of children's progress, especially in the areas of parents' concern.

The box **Creating Two-Way Relationships with Families** summarizes some general guidelines in making such relationships a reality.

Now the star is complete, each point connected to every other point. Creating a community of learners, teaching, curriculum, assessment, and developing relationships with families—all are integral parts of the whole that is early childhood practice.

If you are reading this book, it's very likely that you have a strong desire to contribute to children's lives. To make sure your efforts succeed, you will need to take seriously all five aspects of practice and continually deepen and update your knowledge within each of them. Then the children you teach will learn and thrive.

FAQs

Questions about Developmentally Appropriate Practice

As we talk with teachers, administrators, parents, and policy makers about developmentally appropriate practice, we get asked all sorts of questions. This section covers the most common ones—with the recognition that our responses are always evolving over time. They change as the research base expands but also as a result of the conversations we have with others. We offer these answers, then, not as the "last word" on what are hard questions, but rather to foster further conversations among all early childhood educators.

Is "Developmentally Appropriate Practice" a curriculum?

No, DAP is not a curriculum. It is a set of guidelines that can be used to help educators make decisions about curriculum as well as teaching strategies. *Curriculum* can be defined in many ways, but the most basic definition is usually that curriculum is the *what*—that is, the content (knowledge, skills, and dispositions) to be taught and the plans for experiences through which learning will take place. Planning curriculum that is appropriate for children is certainly one aspect of DAP, but there is not a particular curriculum that is designated as "developmentally appropriate practice."

There are a variety of early childhood curriculum approaches that are based on the underlying principles of child development and learning that undergird the NAEYC guidelines for developmentally appropriate practice. There are also many commercially developed curriculum products that reflect diverse theoretical perspectives on learning and development and provide more or less structure and support for the teacher. Principles of developmentally appropriate practice should always be applied in developing or selecting curriculum.

At the same time, whatever the curriculum model, it can only be truly effective and developmentally appropriate if teachers understand how children learn and develop, and if they adapt their teaching materials, experiences, and strategies to meet those children's individual needs. Curriculum matters, but it does not take the place of a good teacher.

Does DAP mean that there is only one right way to teach?

Actually, developmentally appropriate practice means just the opposite. Individual children vary greatly in their development, prior experience, abilities, preferences, and interests, and there is no formula that works for them all. Moreover, to teach any child effectively, a teacher must use a variety of teaching strategies and make intentional choices about what strategy to use in a particular situation. As we describe in the chapter **Teach to Enhance Development and Learning,** good early childhood teachers acknowledge and encourage, model and demonstrate, create challenges and extend children's thinking, and give specific information and direction (see Bowman, Donovan, & Burns 2000).

Are developmentally appropriate programs unstructured?

The idea that there is very little or no structure in a DAP classroom is a misconception. Again, in reality the opposite is true. To be developmentally appropriate, a program must be thoughtfully structured to build on and advance children's competence. For this reason, a developmentally appropriate program is well organized in its schedule and physical environment and uses a planned curriculum to guide teachers as they assist children to accomplish important learning goals. The structure of a developmentally appropriate program is not rigid, however. Instead it permits adaptation for individual variation and is flexible, so as to accommodate children's interests and progress.

In the DAP classroom, there is a predictable but not rigid schedule to the day, and there are clear rules for acceptable behavior. In the course of the day, children have opportunities to choose from among a number of learning centers and to participate in a variety of other learning contexts, such as large- and small-group times. In all of these contexts, the teacher is intentional in using the environment, materials, and teaching strategies to enable children to acquire important knowledge and skills.

I teach children with disabilities. Won't their learning suffer if I use DAP?

Children with disabilities are children first. They share most of the same developmental and learning needs and have many of the same strengths as their typically developing peers. The DAP principles of meeting children where they are and creating challenging and achievable goals are just as important for children with disabilities. Further, we know from decades of research in early childhood special education that children with disabilities benefit most from being served in inclusive settings, that is, places where they would be found if they did not have a disability (Sandall, McLean, & Smith 2000; Odom et al. 2002).

Teachers of children with identified disabilities should be part of a team that includes specialists and families and that develops and implements an individualized education plan (IEP) for the child. The plan, along with participation in the inclusive setting, should ensure that the child makes desired progress toward the shared goals of the family and the program.

Someone told me that in DAP classrooms, all children do is play. Is that true?

Research shows that self-initiated, teacher-supported play benefits children in many ways. When children play, they engage in many important tasks, such as developing and practicing newly acquired skills, using language, taking turns, making friends, and regulating emotions and behavior according to the demands of the situation. This is why for young children play needs to be a large part of the day—and part of a developmentally appropriate classroom. Moreover, effective teachers often take action to enhance children's play and the learning that goes on in the play context. They engage in one-on-one conversations with children and encourage pretend play with themes, roles, rules, and props—all of which research shows is related to both language and literacy development. (For more on this, see the box **What Good Is Play?** on page 20.)

But play is not the only thing that children do in developmentally appropriate classrooms. Children also work in small groups, listen to stories, meet as a whole group, work on projects, solve problems, participate in developmentally enriching routines, and engage in many other learning experiences.

Is it true that academics have no place in developmentally appropriate early childhood programs?

Academics is a term that is widely used but rarely defined. If academics are understood to mean important foundational skills and knowledge in early literacy, mathematics, science, and other subjects, then academics definitely are an essential part of developmentally appropriate early childhood programs. Of course, to be developmentally appropriate these learning domains must also be addressed in ways that fit children's ways of learning. It is when academics are defined very narrowly as a set of specific facts and when these facts are taught by "drill and kill" or other such methods pushed down from older grades that they are less relevant to young children's overall development and learning.

I need to get my child ready to succeed in school. Doesn't she need more than DAP in her preschool experience?

Developmentally appropriate programs richly contribute to children's learning and development. One of the well-documented research findings about high-quality, developmentally appropriate preschool programs is that they do prepare children to succeed in school, especially children living in poverty (Schweinhart & Weikart 1997; Bowman, Donovan, & Burns 2000). A good

Basics of Developmentally Appropriate Practice

preschool program helps children acquire key knowledge and skills in language, early literacy and mathematics, social and emotional development, and other aspects of school readiness. In fact, if children are not making learning and developmental progress toward important outcomes, then the program is not developmentally appropriate.

My program serves children from a variety of cultures, and I'm wondering whether DAP is the best thing for them. Is DAP for all children or just for some children?

The principles of developmentally appropriate practice call for teachers to pay attention to the social and cultural contexts in which the children live and take these into account in shaping the learning environment. Whatever children's prior experiences or cultural expectations are, teachers help them to make sense of new experiences. At times, this situation will require explicit teaching of the rules or skills that the child has not previously encountered. Or it will require the teacher to recognize that children can acquire the same skills and ideas through different experiences and routines—e.g., children can gain phonological awareness through nursery rhymes, and they can also do so through jump-rope chants. Most important, the classroom must be a welcoming environment that demonstrates respect and support for all children's contexts.

I am sometimes daunted by the learning needs of the children in my Head Start program, and I'm wondering whether DAP will enable them to catch up and be ready for school?

This is a good question, and the answer is "yes, but. . . ." Closing the performance gap between children of low-income families and middle-class families is a formidable task, and it needs to be tackled early in children's lives. Without intervention, differences in children's early environments can be staggering. For instance, a child in a professional family on average hears 11 million words a year, while a child in a welfare family hears just 3 million (Hart & Risley

1995). Most English-language learners also hear far fewer words in English than do their peers from English-speaking homes. Clearly, programs serving low-income children and English-language learners need to give special attention to building children's oral language and vocabulary.

The principles and guidelines of developmentally appropriate practice certainly should underlie all our efforts to serve all these children and their families well. If we truly meet the learners where they are and help them to reach challenging and achievable goals, as DAP requires, we will promote their learning and development to their great long-term benefit. But, as dramatically shown by evidence such as that of Hart and Risley, some children have a lot of ground to make up. So teachers need to be knowledgeable about the learning needs of the children they teach and the teaching strategies with proven success in helping such children reach higher levels of achievement. The **Resources** list provided at the end of this book includes a number of publications (e.g., Burns, Snow, & Griffin 1999; Meier 2004) that will help teachers better understand the educational and developmental needs of children growing up in poverty and the approaches that seem to be most promising in addressing these.

A key fact that should also be noted is that children and families living with the many stresses of poverty typically need access to comprehensive services including health, nutrition, and social services. Outside of Head Start, few children and families receive these services, and this lack makes improving learning and development outcomes that much more difficult. Thus, advocating for these services is important for all those concerned about children's well-being.

I've heard that it is "developmentally inappropriate" to put the alphabet up on a classroom wall or to teach children to read before first grade. Is that true?

This question has become a DAP urban myth. It originated in the context of 1980s schooling, in which first grade expectations were being thrust on preschoolers, and NAEYC's 1987 position statement on DAP called for not teaching letters in isolation. That position statement emphasized teaching letters in the context of meaningful words, such as in children's names or as initial consonants of words children encounter in books or other print materials. From this emphasis the myth of "no alphabet charts" arose.

To clear up such misunderstandings, which were making many early childhood teachers feel they should avoid literacy teaching, NAEYC developed a joint position statement with the International Reading Association called *Learning to Read and Write: Developmentally Appropriate Practices for Young Children* (IRA & NAEYC 1998). Based on decades of research on early literacy and reading, it describes the kinds of preschool literacy outcomes—such as alphabet knowledge, phonological awareness, vocabulary, and concepts of print—that predict later success in learning to read and write. The position paper and accompanying book (Neuman, Copple, & Bredekamp 2000) also describe effective teaching strategies and learning experiences to help children achieve these important outcomes. The statement specifically addresses the question of the alphabet's place in a developmentally appropriate classroom. It states that letters should be where children can see them, touch them, and manipulate them in their work and play. Because learning the alphabet is such a strong predictor of reading, DAP classrooms will certainly have an alphabet on the wall at children's eye level.

As for the second part of the question, developmentally appropriate preschool and kindergarten programs teach children the many important early literacy skills that are precursors to successful reading. With such experiences, some children will become competent readers before first grade; others will not have reached that stage but are making good progress. All children should be provided with the learning experiences that fit where they are and enable them to move forward. To do anything else would be developmentally *in*appropriate.

I teach in a public kindergarten where there is a prescribed curriculum. How can I use DAP in my situation?

You should be able to apply the most fundamental principles of developmentally appropriate practice in every educational setting serving young children. These principles include creating a caring community of learners where everyone feels respected and included; establishing warm, positive relationships with each child; and developing respectful, reciprocal relationships with families. Although some settings and curricula make carrying out these principles more challenging than do others, in virtually all situations teachers will be able to create a positive classroom environment and respectful relationships with children and families.

Of course, developmentally appropriate practice also means getting to know each learner and adapting the curriculum and teaching practices to ensure that children make continual progress in their learning and development. So whatever curriculum a teacher is given, she must adapt it to the needs of the individual children in her class if it is to be developmentally appropriate for them. In some situations, teachers are limited in the flexibility they have to make such adaptations, and having limited flexibility is a loss. But teachers can do some adapting, often more than they might realize—particularly if they become skilled at describing the things they do in their classrooms in terms of the standards or outcomes they are required to meet.

For example, your rationale for having children work together on a project might include "increased opportunity for language use and extended discourse," and you can detail the aspects of literacy, mathematics, science, and other curriculum domains that they will learn from the project. In other words, teachers need to think about how the approaches and learning experiences they want to use with children address the curriculum's prescribed goals and content, and then be able to communicate this rationale to others.

I've heard DAP is about not hurrying children, about giving them the gift of time. Is that right?

The expression "gift of time" comes from a valid concern of not expecting too much of children too soon. But the response of just giving a child time would often do him a real disservice. Why? It isn't just time that promotes human development, it is also what happens while the time passes—the experiences with objects and people the child is having. When the gift of time takes the form of having a child wait a year to enter school, for example, the child might well make less progress out of school than he would in it.

So DAP does not mean simply waiting until children are "ready." It means setting developmentally appropriate expectations and understanding that, although there are some biological limitations, children's learning experiences will drive their development. For example, 2-year-olds and many 3-year-olds lack the fine motor skills needed to manipulate a pencil and form letters, but opportunities to scribble and draw help them get ready to do so. Maturation is needed, but so is experience.

I like to teach in my own style. Doesn't DAP stifle my individuality as a teacher?

Teachers are individuals, just as children are. We each have our own interests, abilities, preferences, social and cultural contexts, and unique experiences that make us who we are. Developmentally appropriate practice calls for the teacher to create a caring community of learners, an important member of which is the teacher. Teachers should bring their unique selves, including their talents and interests, into the classroom. If a teacher is artistic, musical, literary, athletic, or whatever, she should be able to draw on her own style in her teaching, because it probably reflects her strengths (see, e.g., Alati 2005, in **Resources**). The important thing to remember is not every child will share the teacher's preferred style. To be effective, you must understand how the *children* learn and develop, and use a variety of strategies to meet those children's individual needs.

I think DAP makes sense, but the families I serve have different ideas about how their children should be taught. What should I do?

Begin by dropping the jargon when you communicate with families. Don't talk about "DAP" or even "developmentally appropriate practice." Instead, have a conversation with families about your learning goals for their child and their goals.

Negotiating differences begins with you clearly understanding your own preferences and where they come from. This might take your doing some serious thinking and reflecting first. Then communicate about your point of view and listen, truly *listen,* to the family's concerns. When you and the family articulate your respective goals, it is likely that you can find common ground. Be open to learning from family members and willing to expand your view of effective, developmentally appropriate practice based on what you learn. In a successful negotiation, families also learn and change. If you just give in to parents' demands, you will lose self-respect and probably effectiveness; if parents just give in to your position, they lose their power in their relationship with you and in their children's lives. In either case, children ultimately lose. The goal is a win-win outcome in which teacher and family learn from each other and come up with a solution that works for both.

Isn't DAP too "easy" for children once they get to kindergarten or first grade?

What is developmentally appropriate varies with the age, experience, and abilities of the children. So, in developmentally appropriate kindergarten and first grade classrooms, the expectations and outcomes will not be "too easy" for those 5-, 6-, or 7-year-old children (see, e.g., Gullo in press). Rather, the expectations and outcomes of the programs will continue to be achievable but also challenging. For instance, conventional reading—the ability to gain meaning from unfamiliar text—may be an inappropriate expectation for most preschoolers to meet, but it is certainly developmentally appropriate for most first-graders.

Where can I get more information about DAP?

This book is an introduction to the basics of DAP. A more detailed description of the principles and concepts is NAEYC's *Developmentally Appropriate Practice in Early Childhood Programs* (Bredekamp & Copple 1997). Also, a list of many useful resources for understanding and using developmentally appropriate practice appears in the **Resources** section at the end of this book.

A Changing Picture: Children at 3, 4, and 5

The following charts give a general picture of what children are like in the preschool and kindergarten years—from age 3 through 5—and how adults can promote their learning and development.

For each age group we have divided the common characteristics and behaviors into four categories of development (physical, intellectual, social, emotional). But in doing so, we do not mean to imply that the different areas don't overlap, because certainly they do. Likewise, there is considerable overlap between the age groups. Some children will exhibit certain characteristics and behaviors at earlier ages than their peers; others will take longer to acquire a given set of skills and concepts.

In other words, generalizations are only that. It is through close observation and interaction with the individual children in their classrooms that skilled teachers assess where children are and so know how to best guide them.

Children at 3

What children are like	How adults can help
Physical development	
Children love to use their large muscles. They become stronger and their balance and movement control improve greatly during the year. They are able to alternate feet when climbing stairs, jump, do a forward somersault, and kick a ball.	Provide climbers, tricycles, balls, and lots of space and time to run, jump, and gallop. Demonstrate new skills or provide assistance and feedback as children take on new challenges.
Children are able to manipulate a paintbrush and implements such as crayons, markers, and thick pencils. Their scribbles become more controlled and deliberate. They can stack blocks to create a short-to-medium tower. Children this age may also spill food or art supplies sometimes, but their control and coordination are improving. They become more able to unbutton and unzip as their small-muscle skills improve.	Materials such as pegboards, beads to string, and construction sets are beneficial. Blocks are engaging and useful for developing eye-hand coordination, as are finger plays. Offer materials with which children can practice pouring, rolling, squeezing—these will build strength in their hand muscles.
Children are increasingly able to engage in self-care activities such as hand washing, dressing, and toileting, but accidents may happen occasionally. Boys may not be as advanced as girls in toilet learning.	Children can help with dressing and undressing, but still need assistance. Be patient, and treat accidents matter-of-factly. Have extra clothes on hand. Ask children to help clean up and to change their own clothes.

What children are like	How adults can help
Intellectual development	
Children often spend relatively long times at tasks they choose—e.g., playing in sand, building with blocks, painting, following an obstacle course, engaging in dramatic play. They may ride a tricycle for long periods, or do the same puzzle three times in a row. Children will test their skills, and may repeat activities over and over again.	Plan the schedule to allow large blocks of time for independent activity. Offer a wide range of learning experiences and materials.
Children this age are curious. They want to experiment with cause and effect. They take things apart with glee.	Provide them with materials for their investigations—e.g., blocks, sand, and water (with cups to pour and other tools), puzzles, and things that come apart.
They can identify common colors such as yellow, red, blue, and green. They can often recognize and identify a few basic shapes, most particularly circles and squares.	Encourage them to match and sort colors, shapes, and textures. Play games such as "What's furry?" "Can you point to the circle in this picture?" and "I see something red. Can you find it?" Use relevant vocabulary in everyday conversation ("I see you're wearing your new red jacket again today").
Counting becomes more precise, although children this age might not yet have learned correct number labels. Three-year-olds can recognize the number in very small groups of objects, and by age 4 children can recognize *(cont.)*	Provide ample opportunities for counting, including counting games. If possible, move items one at a time while counting. Incorporate counting words naturally into conversation—talking about "three crayons" *(cont.)*

3-Year-Olds, cont.

What children are like	How adults can help
that the last number in a sequence represents the total quantity of items in a group. At age 3, they are interested in quantity and readily understand *more*.	instead of "the crayons" is an easy and effective way to increase children's interest and knowledge of number.
Vocabularies grow rapidly, ranging at this age between 2,000 and 4,000 words. Children can talk so that 75–80 percent of their speech is intelligible, and they understand much more than they speak. They use complete sentences of three to five words and employ words to describe and explain. If they are regularly exposed to two languages, children are likely to acquire facility in both.	Provide lots of conversation opportunities for children to hear and use language in its many uses and forms—e.g., poems, nursery rhymes, recordings, games, stories. Allow plenty of time for children to speak. Talk with each child every day. Give clear but not too lengthy explanations to children's questions. Use both English and, if you are able, the child's home language. Encourage bilingualism, and talk to children in English at a little higher level than they talk to you. Help children with comprehension by using props, non-verbal cues, simplified speech, and repetition.
Children begin to understand that words can be spoken and then written down to be read again. Children will try to make marks on paper that resemble writing ("This is my name, Bill")— some of which may approximate real letters— and they enjoy scribbling.	Have children tell you a story that you write down for them. They then might want to illustrate it. Sometimes children will draw first, then ask you to write their story. Provide crayons and markers for children to experiment making marks with.

3-Year-Olds, cont.

What children are like	How adults can help
Children can listen to longer stories and will pretend to read themselves. They can predict what might happen in the story and connect it to their own life experiences.	Read aloud to small groups (four to six children) every day; talk with children before, during, and after the story. Gradually increase the length and complexity of the stories you read and tell.
They enjoy repeating words, sounds, and tunes. They begin to recognize musical melodies, match a few tones, and move in reasonably good time to music.	Provide musical experiences in which children participate by singing, playing, and dancing. Select music from many cultures.
Social development	
Young 3-year-olds prefer to play alongside another child or with one or two others.	Have many individual activities and materials that children can do side by side. Also offer some things that require cooperation. Offer materials such as dramatic play props that encourage interactive play. Some children may need help learning how to play with others.
Friendships are beginning but are often short-lived, especially among younger 3-year-olds.	Support children's friendships. One good way is to help children treat each other as friends. Talk about things good friends do for each other, and read books with children that feature friendships.

What children are like	How adults can help
Children may share when given the opportunity. Sometimes they can wait for a short while for a turn. Children can use their newfound language skills to voice their feelings during conflicts with others, and may be able to voice solutions to problems. However, they may still resort to physical aggression.	Allow sharing to develop spontaneously; forcing it will not work. Children share when others are generous with them and when they do not feel the need to protect their possessions. Equip children with skills for dealing with classroom problems by themselves ("Use words to tell Daryl that you are playing with the truck now. He can have a turn later"). Model language when necessary.
Emotional development	
Children develop a firm sense of their sex, age, race, language, and culture. They are beginning to develop a sense of self-concept—an understanding of their own unique characteristics. By age 3½ they will be able to describe key attributes about themselves.	Share children's pride in who they are. Respect each child. Incorporate their home languages, cultural objects, and familiar activities as a natural part of every day.
	Be aware that a child's growing sense of self can lead to increased possessiveness over objects. You can acknowledge this possessiveness while encouraging social interaction through compromise ("Yes, Henry, you are playing with the truck right now. Mara also would like a turn. In a little while, can she have a turn?").
Older 3-year-olds tend to be affectionate with younger children. They often begin to have special friends they are fond of.	Encourage children to talk about their feelings and to describe them to others. They may have some awareness that other people experience things differently, but this understanding is still difficult. Model compassionate and caring behavior.

3-Year-Olds, cont.

What children are like	How adults can help
Children are learning to trust the important adults in their lives. They are now more independent and take pride in new skills. When upset, however, they may revert to toddler behaviors.	Separation from parents can still be painful for children this age and they may cry when parents leave. Respect their feelings and comfort them with reassuring words and hugs. Tell the child about when the parent will return ("Mommy will pick you up after nap time today").
Three-year-olds like to be treated as older children at times, but they still have difficulty regulating their own behavior. They may still put objects in their mouths that can be dangerous, or wander off if not carefully supervised. The delightful, silly sense of humor they possess can sometimes get out of control. Children may occasionally still have tantrums.	Children this age need close supervision and positive reinforcement. If they say something that is offensive or hurtful to others, try to explain how their friends' feelings have been hurt. Tantrums should largely be ignored; acknowledge the child's feelings verbally, but do not let children use tantrums to manipulate.
Children express intense feelings, such as fear and affection. New fears often develop at this age—e.g., children may be afraid of things they've imagined, such as monsters under the bed, or of unfamiliar people or characters they encounter. Loud noises can also be frightening.	Take children's fears seriously—e.g., for a small child, a clown may be seen as an enormous threat. Provide physical reassurance by allowing the child to cling to you. Offer reassuring words. Using a puppet with children can be helpful—the puppet can talk about something he's afraid of, and children can offer advice, prompted by your questions.

Source: The information in this chart was primarily adapted from Day 2004, 65–78; additional sources include Bredekamp & Copple 1997; Schickedanz 1999; Miller 2001; Essa 2002; and Berk 2004.

Basics of Developmentally Appropriate Practice

Children at 4

What children are like	How adults can help
Physical development	
The child's repertoire of large-muscle skills is expanding, and skills are becoming more refined. Skipping and hopping may appear. Children are good at riding tricycles. Children can bounce and catch a ball, jump over a low obstacle, and balance on one foot.	Allow plenty of opportunities for children to use their large-muscle skills—e.g., obstacle courses, climbing structures, large hollow blocks. Demonstrate new physical skills and provide just the right amount of assistance as children try out new challenges on their own.
Small muscles gain coordination. Children can use scissors, glue, small beads, and paint-brushes with more skill. Cutting and pasting become favorite activities. Their creations begin to resemble real objects.	Continue to offer a variety of art materials and blank paper. Let children cut and draw what they choose rather than following lines printed in a coloring book or worksheet. Provide materials that call for more eye-hand coordination, such as sewing cards and smaller beads to string. Use more difficult finger plays.
Children can use a fork effectively to feed themselves, and with adult supervision can use a knife to cut soft foods. They can usually dress and undress independently. Some children may be able to tie their own shoes as they approach age 5.	Be patient with children who are mastering self-care skills. Offer assistance as needed, but give children room to manage for themselves.
Intellectual development	
Children are increasingly able to carry over projects and topics of study from one day to the next. They enjoy writing for real purposes such as messages to friends. Artwork takes on *(cont.)*	Plan projects that engage children's thinking. Have children make meaningful signs—e.g., a special block construction could be labeled with a child's name and a request to *(cont.)*

4-Year-Olds, cont.

What children are like	How adults can help
new meaning, and they may want to save their finished products.	leave the structure standing for a day or two. Children can sign their work, and it can be kept in a safe place or displayed.
Children are increasingly able to figure out how things work and fit together. They are curious; they want to try different ways to do things and to use different types of hand tools. They can sort objects using more than two categories.	Offer all kinds of objects for children to explore—e.g., an old toaster with any dangerous parts removed or clock or anything else safe for eager learners. Introduce more complicated projects and new types of tools, such as a computer or new carpentry tools. Ask children to think of a variety of ways to solve problems ("How could you get the water from this side to that side using the things we have here?"). Involve children in making repairs. Stock up on paste and glue!
Children are naturally interested in shapes, colors, and textures. Most children can name six to eight colors and a few typical shapes, such as circles, squares, and triangles, by age 4.	Use the names of shapes (in both two- and three-dimensions) and colors in natural ways ("This triangle block might make a good roof for your house," "Your red shoes match the red balloon in this picture"). Provide many textures through cooking, woodworking, clay, finger paint, and dress-up clothes.
Children learn to count to 20 and beyond, and may be interested in printing numbers. They compare sizes and weights of objects.	Encourage the use of number and quantity in real experiences such as measuring, distributing or dividing items, and matching. Lead children in counting and comparing in each of the languages spoken by the group.

Basics of Developmentally Appropriate Practice

4-Year-Olds, cont.

What children are like	How adults can help
Given sufficient language exposure in their home and school environments, children have 4,000 to 6,000 words in their vocabularies. They are capable of speaking in five- to six-word sentences. Children are persistent in asking "Why?"	Invite children to tell their own stories, and allow ample time for them to talk among themselves and with you about what they are doing. Encourage children to use varied ways to find answers to questions: asking people, reading books, experimenting.
Extended conversations are now possible, sentences become more complex, and children understand more words than they speak. Children who speak multiple languages use both with ease and switch between them.	Engage children in extended conversation, i.e., with five or more turn-taking exchanges. Provide many materials and experiences such as field trips for children to gain new knowledge and vocabulary. For English-language learners and their classmates, offer positive models of people speaking the children's home languages and of their cultures. Communicate with parents about the need to support the home language.
Interest in written and spoken language increases. Experimentation with written marks continues; letter-like forms and a few actual letters may appear. Children learn the names of letters, recognize some words, and are interested in print. They begin to match letters with those in their names and other words they want to write, becoming aware of the discrete sounds that make up spoken language and that can be manipulated.	Provide a print-rich environment with books and other materials in several languages for children to use. Respond to children's questions about letters and words. Write down the stories children tell you. Encourage children to write their own names and other words, giving help as they ask for it but not "correcting" their spelling. Draw their attention to letters and letter sounds ("That red sign starts with *S*—does anyone know what it says?"). Help children sound out words they are trying to write. Keep paper and pencils or markers in all learning centers for children to use.

What children are like	How adults can help
Children enjoy making up their own stories, which are usually a mixture of make-believe and real. When retelling long stories they are increasingly able to get the main points of the narrative right.	Give children a chance to use the flannel board, puppets, or other dramatic play methods to recreate stories. Invite children to retell stories to the group. Encourage children to talk about past, future, or imaginary events. Take care not to use stories that contain stereotypes.
Children like singing games, want to dramatize songs, and make up their own songs. They are increasingly able to sing melodies on pitch and move in time to the beat.	Offer a range of musical and rhythmic experiences including games and songs with rhymes and other phonological features. Include selections with words in other languages, more complicated actions, and more real instruments from other cultures.
Social development	
Children show interest in others, and spend time watching. They love to play together with two or three others. They also still need time alone.	Provide lots of small-group, child-directed activities. Have a quiet, private space where children can go to be by themselves. Keep whole-group activities within children's span of interest, usually 20 minutes or less.
Children develop strong friendships and strongly desire playmates. Friendships with one other child are flexible but longer lasting; these friendships are often with those of the same sex. Children's ideas of friendship evolve from moment to moment, and they may use promises to manipulate one another (e.g., "I'll *(cont.)*	Encourage children's special relationships, but intervene in a sensitive manner when children exclude others or exhibit jealous behaviors. Incorporating additional children into a triad of squabbling children may defuse power struggles. Because children's friendships are becoming more obvious, it is also easier *(cont.)*

What children are like	How adults can help
be your friend if you give me that ball"). They can be jealous of their friends' attention toward others, and may also exclude other children from play in order to guard their special friendships.	for teachers to identify which children are neglected or rejected by peers. Teachers should assist these children by pairing them with others for activities and coaching them to enter play. Read picture books with children about friendships, and talk to them about being a good friend.
Children are increasingly able to follow a leader or act as a leader.	Children can be leaders and followers naturally throughout the day—e.g., during dramatic play, outdoors, on field trips, and during music.
Sharing and taking turns are becoming more common. At times children are able to resolve differences and negotiate conflicts between themselves with words. Younger 4-year-olds still find cooperating and sharing a challenge. At times children use their growing language ability in an aggressive way ("You can't come to my birthday party!"). Children gradually have fewer disagreements and are often quick to apologize for their behavior.	By the end of this age period, children will cooperate in taking turns and sharing much of the time *if* adults model cooperative, generous behavior and do not push sharing before children are ready. Encourage children to use words to work out problems that arise during play. Acknowledge and encourage spontaneous sharing, and create opportunities for cooperation as well.
Emotional development	
Children are curious about differences and similarities in people and how they live.	Help children understand how people are alike and different—in physical characteristics, family styles, and culture—and that each of us is special and valuable. Treat children with respect so they will do the same *(cont.)*

What children are like	How adults can help
Prejudices may arise unless children are helped to appreciate one another and to recognize what is fair for everyone.	with others, and talk about differences and differently abled people in an honest, nonfrightening way. Displays and materials throughout the room should include art, music, and authentic everyday objects from a variety of cultures. Discuss what is fair and accurate (e.g., sharing songs drawn from a specific culture) and what isn't (e.g., playing "Cowboys and Indians," stereotyped drawings in books).
Children are developing real empathy with each other, and friendships are longer lasting.	Show empathy and consideration with children and acknowledge them when they demonstrate their understanding of how others feel. Support friendships, and model the behavior you expect from children.
Children this age are increasingly capable of caring for themselves. They are usually able to say goodbye to their parents with little diffi-culty if they have had previous group experi-ence. They want to take more responsibility and like to use and do adult things. Children have definite preferences. While they are easily encouraged, they are easily discouraged as well and need positive reinforcement.	Allow children to handle responsibilities they are capable of (e.g., pour their own juice, wash their hands, hang up their coats by themselves). Watch and talk to each child individually every day to gain information about what he or she can do. Offer real objects for children to use and play with. Respect children's preferences, and support their internal motivation to do well— rewards are not needed beyond children's own sense that they are trying and making progress.

Basics of Developmentally Appropriate Practice

4-Year-Olds, cont.

What children are like	How adults can help
Children are gaining greater ability to regulate their own behavior. They can wait for short periods of time and have more respect for one another's belongings. They may also be silly and boisterous. Sometimes they will use inappropriate language.	Continue to help children control their own behavior. Plan the day so waiting is not excessive. Use children's humor (e.g., riddles and nonsense words can be fun). Don't reward bathroom language by giving children who use it lots of attention. Explain that those words are not used in your program.
Children may still need an adult to help them manage their strong feelings of fear, anger, and frustration. Children are still trying to understand what is real and what is make-believe, and their imaginations may create new fears.	Accept children's feelings and help them find a safe way to express them ("You are angry that your tower was knocked over. Let's sit here for a while until you feel calm enough to talk with the children who wrecked it"). Children's books may help them see how others have faced and resolved problems such as divorce, moving, death, disabilities, learning a new language, or accepting a new baby in the family. Talk with children about what can really happen and what is just pretend.

Source: The information in this chart was primarily adapted from Day 2004, 65–78; additional sources include Bredekamp & Copple 1997; Schickedanz 1999; Miller 2001; Essa 2002; and Berk 2004.

Children at 5

What children are like	How adults can help
Physical development	
Children can skip, walk backwards quickly, balance securely on a two-inch beam, jump down several steps, hop confidently, and usually have developed mature throwing and catching skills. They love to show off their physical prowess.	Children enjoy catching games, which can be adapted for varying ability levels by using bigger or smaller balls and varying throwing styles. They still need close supervision, especially when attempting daring tricks with their newfound abilities.
Interest in activities involving fine motor skills increases with children's refined abilities. Children become increasingly skilled in activities such as drawing and cutting and pasting. Manipulation of writing instruments improves with increased hand-eye coordination. By this age it is usually obvious whether children are right- or left-handed.	Art activities are popular with 5-year-olds. Allow children to experiment with art forms and materials; do not make critical comments on the "right" way to represent something. Continue to offer many kinds of art materials; introduce a variety of art processes, such as collage, watercolors, and printing. Offer both right- and left-handed scissors.
Children can help with food preparation and setup, and can largely dress themselves. Many children will master shoe tying by age 6. Children enjoy being able to do such things on their own.	Allow children to serve themselves at the table. Continue to offer assistance as needed with dressing if children need occasional help, such as with shoe tying. Offer children some privacy with toileting, but remind them to wash their hands.

Basics of Developmentally Appropriate Practice

5-Year-Olds, cont.

What children are like	How adults can help
Intellectual development	
Children often engage in activities with a result or end product in mind. They are gaining in ability to plan ahead.	Involve children in brainstorming class projects and activities. Allow them to revisit earlier work and to judge for themselves when something is finished. Ask children about the activities they are involved with. Challenge them to experiment and to solve problems, to think about what will happen next, and to review their work.
Children continue to enjoy hands-on exploration and learning. Their observational skills are increasing, and they are more likely to connect related information.	Provide a stimulating environment with many hands-on activities. Give children time and space for exploration. Foster children's initiative and sustained engagement. Support age-appropriate risk taking, within safe boundaries.
Children's understanding of shapes is still rather global. They can learn about the different parts of shapes and how they fit together, and some older 5-year-olds may be able to grasp isolated geometric attributes (e.g., "a square has four equal sides"). Children have a good understanding of basic colors.	Provide varied examples of shapes, colors in different contexts, and textures. Offer art experiences such as collage so children can experiment with different textures, colors, and shapes. Model how shapes can be slid, flipped, and rotated yet remain the same shape. Have children make shapes using toothpicks or straws for sides. Provide shape puzzles, such as tangrams, for children to experiment with. Encourage children to make patterns with shapes and colors.

5-Year-Olds, cont.

What children are like	How adults can help
Children can count flexibly to solve a variety of problems, including those that involve number (counting), addition, and subtraction.	Continue to incorporate number into everyday activities, such as setting the table with the correct number of place settings or counting the number of spaces to move in a game. Play games that compare small groups of objects or symbols.
Vocabularies continue to increase; children can use between 5,000 and 8,000 words. Children use fuller, more complex sentences and take turns in conversation. Children's questions become more relevant to topics at hand. They have mastered most of the grammatical structures to which they are regularly exposed.	Answer children's questions when possible; encourage them to find out more through other means. Ask them questions in turn to expand their thinking.
Children are gaining ability to match letters to sounds. Some will begin to read during this year. Writing skill varies with experience; most children will be able to string a few actual letters together, creating a few short words such as *mom, dad*, or their own first names. Children often continue to use letter-like forms and scribble writing as well.	Take advantage of opportunities to highlight letters and sounds in the environment. Plenty of paper and marking tools throughout the classroom will encourage spontaneous exploration. Children may ask for help in creating individual letters; your writing out each line segment of a letter in a different color may help children understand how letters are formed.
With practice, children can tell and retell stories. They enjoy repeating stories, poems, and songs, as well as acting out plays or stories.	Encourage children to record and enact their stories in different ways. Children's stories can be written down by an adult, children can act out stories in the dramatic play area, and favorite stories can be illustrated.

Basics of Developmentally Appropriate Practice

5-Year-Olds, cont.

What children are like	How adults can help
Children know the words to many poems and songs and enjoy singing. They love to play with words.	Enjoy singing silly songs and exploring funny poetry that plays with language, such as selections from Shel Silverstein and Dr. Seuss. Provide a wide range of music activities, including exposure to an array of rhythm instruments. Children will enjoy playing "orchestra."
Social development	
Children this age like cooperative play, often enjoying the company of one or two special friends at a time. Children love dramatic play with others; they also like to act out others' roles and show off in front of new people. They may also joke and tease to get attention. But, they may become shy at times.	Plan the day and the classroom environment to encourage cooperative play opportunities—i.e., provide ample time for creative and dramatic play as well as a variety of play props and cooperative activities. Plan many opportunities for flexible small-group work.
They can maintain friendships. They yearn for friendship and respect from their peers, made all the more precious by their newfound social powers of exclusion and snubbing. Pairs and small groups of children enjoy playing together for extended periods of time. They may, however, exclude peers. Children understand the power of rejecting others and may verbally threaten to end friendships or select others.	Developing the social skills needed to maintain relationships is not automatic; children do need coaching, supervision, and modeling of prosocial behaviors. Check in with children from time to time, guiding them to use positive ways of dealing with others. Model inclusive and friendly language. If particular children are continually picked on, it may be because they lack play skills—perhaps a child is bossy, or not very observant as to the play themes others are engaged in. In these cases you may be able to coach children in social skills.

5-Year-Olds, cont.

What children are like	How adults can help
Children can cooperate well, take turns, and share, although there may be times they do not wish to. They also recognize the rights of others to a turn and may stand up for them. On occasion, children will take others' things and then lie about it. They are so eager to be good that they don't like to admit when they've done wrong.	Use verbal encouragement to foster and recognize prosocial behavior. When children have difficulty resolving conflicts on their own, wait until they have calmed down and, at an appropriate time, coach them on specific language and strategies to use.
Emotional development	
Children continue to explore differences and similarities between themselves and others. They are still primarily egocentric, however, understanding the world through their own point of view. Same-sex friendships become stronger (especially for boys), and children may choose gender-stereotypical activities.	Model acceptance of others' differences, and expose children to information about different kinds of people. Provide a variety of activities, and challenge children's thinking. Encourage the play styles of both girls and boys, and accept individual differences.
Children enjoy others and can behave in a warm and empathetic manner.	Continue to model kindness and empathy. When children exclude or snub others, work with the group to foster understanding of how it feels to be hurt. In one-to-one situations, or with a few children, invite the snubbed child to describe her feelings.

5-Year-Olds, cont.

What children are like	How adults can help
Children this age take responsibility seriously. Within limits they are independent, competent, and reliable and can usually assess their own capabilities with accuracy.	They enjoy being helpers and are proud to have special roles and tasks in the classroom. Allow children to choose activities, when possible. Having significant blocks of time for child-initiated activities will allow children to complete projects to their satisfaction and thus foster a sense of accomplishment and competence.
Children are capable of being quite well-behaved and polite. They are more self-contained and show more control. They generally are good judges of what they can and cannot do.	Your attentive listening and responsiveness will reinforce their good behavior. When children do lose control, a short period away from other children may help them regain composure, but time-out as a punishment is not an effective approach.
Children also have strong feelings, and fears may increase with increased imaginative skills. They still confuse fantasy with reality on occasion. Increasing awareness of the world may introduce scary realities.	Reassure children when they are afraid, and take their concerns seriously. Adults need to limit children's exposure to media that may be overwhelming or inappropriate. When traumatic events occur—whether in a child's family or in the world at large—children need to be reassured that it is in no way the child's fault.

Source: The information in this chart was adapted from Bredekamp & Copple 1997; Schickedanz 1999; Miller 2001; Essa 2002; Berk 2004; and Day 2004.

References

Berk, L. 2004. *Infants and children: Prenatal through middle childhood.* 5th ed. Boston, MA: Allyn and Bacon.

Bodrova, E., & D.J. Leong. 2003. Chopsticks and counting chips: Do play and foundational skills need to compete for the teacher's attention in an early childhood classroom? *Young Children* 58 (3): 10–17.

Bowman, B.T., M.S. Donovan, & M.S. Burns, eds. 2000. *Eager to learn: Educating our preschoolers.* Washington, DC: National Academies Press. Available online: www.nap.edu.

Bredekamp, S., & C. Copple, eds. 1997. *Developmentally appropriate practice in early childhood programs.* Rev. ed. Washington, DC: NAEYC.

Copley, J.V. 2000. *The young child and mathematics.* Washington, DC: NAEYC.

Davidson, J. 1996. *Emergent literacy and dramatic play in early education.* Albany, NY: Delmar.

Day, C.B., ed. 2004. *Essentials for child development associates working with young children.* Washington, DC: Council for Professional Recognition.

Essa, E. 2002. *Introduction to early childhood education.* 4th ed. Clifton Park, NY: Thompson Delmar Learning.

Gestwicki, C. 1999. *Developmentally appropriate practice, curriculum, and development in early education.* Clifton Park, NY: Thomson Delmar Learning.

Gullo, D.F., ed. In press. *K today: Teaching and learning in the kindergarten year.* Washington, DC: NAEYC.

Hart, C.H., D.C. Burts, & R. Charlesworth. 1997. Integrated developmentally appropriate curriculum: From theory and research to practice. In *Integrated curriculum and developmentally appropriate practice*, eds. C. Hart, D. Burts, & R. Charlesworth., 1–27. Albany, NY: State University of New York Press.

Hart, B., & T. Risley. 1995. *Meaningful differences in everyday parenting and intellectual development in young American children*. Baltimore: Paul H. Brookes.

Hills, T.W. 1992. Reaching potentials through appropriate assessment. In *Reaching potentials, vol. 1: Appropriate curriculum and assessment for young children*, eds. S. Bredekamp & T. Rosegrant, 43–63. Washington, DC: NAEYC.

IRA (International Reading Association) & NAEYC. 1998. *Learning to read and write: Developmentally appropriate practices for young children*. Joint Position Statement. Washington, DC: NAEYC. Also available online: www.naeyc.org/about/positions/pdf/PSREAD98.pdf.

Jablon, J.R., A.L. Dombro, & M.O. Dichtelmiller. 1999. *The power of observation*. Washington, DC: Teaching Strategies.

Jones, E., & G. Reynolds. 1992. *The play's the thing: Teachers' roles in children's play*. New York: Teachers College Press.

Kamii, C., & R. DeVries. 1980. *Group games in early education: Implications of Piaget's theory*. Washington, DC: NAEYC.

Kostelnik, M.J., A.K. Soderman, & A.P. Whiren. 1999. *Developmentally appropriate curriculum: Best practices in early childhood education*. 2d ed. Upper Saddle River, NJ: Prentice Hall.

Landry, S.H. 2005. *Effective early childhood programs: Turning knowledge into action*. Houston, TX: University of Texas, Health Science Center.

Leong, D.J. 2004. Personal communication.

Marulis, L.M. 2000. Anti-bias teaching to address cultural diversity. *Multicultural Education* 7 (3): 27–31.

McAfee, O., D.J. Leong, & E. Bodrova. 2004. *Basics of assessment: A primer for early childhood educators*. Washington, DC: NAEYC.

Miller, K. 2001. *Ages and stages: Developmental descriptions and activities, birth through eight years*. Rev. ed. West Palm Beach, FL: Telshare.

NAEYC. 1995. Responding to linguistic and cultural diversity: Recommendations for effective early childhood education. Position Statement. Washington, DC: Author. Also available online: www.naeyc.org/about/positions/PSDIV98.asp.

NAEYC. 1996. Developmentally appropriate practice in early childhood programs serving children from birth through age 8. Position Statement. Washington, DC: Author. Also available online: www.naeyc.org/about/positions/pdf/PSDAP98.pdf.

NAEYC. 2005a. Screening and assessment of young English-language learners (supplement, to the NAEYC position statement on early childhood curriculum, assessment, and program evaluation). Washington, DC: Author. Also available online: www.naeyc.org/about/positions/pdf/ELL_Supplement.pdf.

NAEYC. 2005b. *NAEYC Early Childhood Program Standards and Accreditation Criteria: The mark of quality in early childhood education.* Washington, DC: Author. Also available online: www.naeyc.org/accreditation/next_era.asp.

NAEYC & NAECS/SDE (National Association of Early Childhood Specialists in State Departments of Education). 2003. Early childhood curriculum, assessment, and program evaluation: Building an effective, accountable system in programs for children birth to age 8. Joint Position Statement. Washington, DC: Author. Available online: www.naeyc.org/about/positions/pdf/pscape.pdf.

Neuman, S.B., C. Copple, & S. Bredekamp. 2000. *Learning to read and write: Developmentally appropriate practices for young children.* Washington DC: NAEYC.

Odom, L.L., R. Wolery, J. Lieber, & E. Horn. 2002. *Widening the circle: Including children with disabilities in preschool programs.* New York: Teachers College Press.

Pianta, R.C. 2000. *Enhancing relationships between children and teachers.* Washington, DC: American Psychological Association.

Sandall, S., M.E. McLean, & B.J. Smith. 2000. *DEC recommended practices in early intervention/early childhood special education.* Denver, CO: Division for Early Childhood (DEC) of the Council for Exceptional Children (CEC).

Sawyers, J.K., & C.S. Rogers. 1988. *Helping young children develop through play.* Washington, DC: NAEYC.

Schickedanz, J. 1999. *Much more than the ABCs: The early stages of reading and writing.* Washington, DC: NAEYC.

Schweinhart, L.J., & D.P. Weikart. 1997. The High/Scope preschool curriculum comparison study through age 23. *Early Childhood Research Quarterly* 12 (2).

Shonkoff, J.P., & D.A. Phillips, eds. 2000. *From neurons to neighborhoods: The science of early childhood development.* Washington, DC: National Academies Press. Available online: www.nap.edu.

Smilansky, S. 1990. Sociodramatic play: Its relevance to behavior and achievement in schools. In *Children's play and learning: Perspectives and policy implications,* eds. E. Klugman & S. Smilansky, 18–42. New York: Teachers College Press.

Stone, J.G. 2001. *Building classroom community: The early childhood teacher's role.* Washington, DC: NAEYC.

U.S. Department of Health and Human Services. 2003, September. *The Head Start leaders guide to positive child outcomes.* Washington, DC: Administration for Children, Youth and Families, Head Start Bureau.

Vygotsky, L.S. [1934] 1986. *Thought and language.* Cambridge, MA: MIT Press.

Resources

Alati, S. 2005. What about our passions as teachers? Incorporating individual interests in emergent curricula. *Young Children* 60 (6): 86–89.

Aronson, S.S., ed. 2002. *Healthy young children: A manual for programs.* 4th ed. Washington, DC: NAEYC.

Bardige, B.S., & M.M. Segal. 2005. *Building literacy with love: A guide for teachers and caregivers of children birth through age 5.* Washington, DC: Zero to Three.

Bowman, B., ed. 2002. *Love to read.* Washington, DC: National Black Child Development Institute.

Bredekamp, S., & C. Copple, eds. 1997. *Developmentally appropriate practice in early childhood programs.* Rev. ed. Washington, DC: NAEYC.

Bright Horizons Family Solutions. 2003. *Ready to respond: Emergency preparedness plan for early care and education centers.* Available online: www.brighthorizons.com/talktochildren/archive_old_site/emergency_plan.doc.

Bronson, M.B. 1995. *The right stuff for children birth to 8: Selecting play materials to support development.* Washington, DC: NAEYC.

Burns, M.S., P. Griffin, & C.E. Snow, eds. 1999. *Starting out right: A guide to promoting children's reading success.* Washington, DC: National Academies Press. Available online: www.nap.edu.

Basics of Developmentally Appropriate Practice

Burns, M.S., C.E. Snow, & P. Griffin, eds. 1999. *Starting out right: A guide to promoting children's reading success.* Washington, DC: National Academies Press. Available online: www.nap.edu.

Butterfield, P.M., C.A. Martin, & A.P. Prairie. 2004. *Emotional connections: How relationships guide early learning.* Washington, DC: Zero to Three.

Copley, J.V. 2000. *The young child and mathematics.* Washington, DC: NAEYC.

Davidson, J. 1996. *Emerging literacy and dramatic play in early education.* Albany, NY: Delmar.

Day, C.B., ed. 2004. *Essentials for child development associates working with young children.* Washington, DC: Council for Professional Recognition.

Derman-Sparks, L., & the ABC Task Force. 1989. *Anti-bias curriculum: Tools for empowering young children.* Washington, DC: NAEYC.

Dever, M.T., C. Kessenich, & R.C. Falconer. 2003. Implementing developmentally appropriate practices in a developmentally inappropriate climate: Assessment in kindergarten. *Dimensions of Early Childhood* 31 (3): 27–33.

Dickinson, D.K., & P.O. Tabors. 2001. *Beginning literacy with language: Young children learning at home and school.* Baltimore, MD: Paul H. Brookes.

Diffily, D., & K. Morrison, eds. 1996. *Family-friendly communication for early childhood programs.* Washington, DC: NAEYC.

Dodge, D.T., L.J. Colker, & C. Heroman. 2000. *Connecting content, teaching, and learning.* Washington, DC: Teaching Strategies.

Dodge, D.T., L.J. Colker, & C. Heroman. 2002. *The creative curriculum for preschool.* 4th ed. Washington, DC: Teaching Strategies.

Dragan, P.B. 2005. *A how-to guide for teaching English language learners in the primary classroom.* Portsmouth, NH: Heinemann.

Dunn, L., & S. Kontos. 1997. What have we learned about developmentally appropriate practice? *Young Children* 52 (5): 4–13.

Eggers-Piérola, C. 2005. *Connections and commitments: Reflecting Latino values in early childhood programs.* Portsmouth, NH: Heinemann.

Egley, E.H., & R.J. Egley. 2000. Teaching principals, parents, and colleagues about developmentally appropriate practice. *Young Children* 55 (5): 48–51.

Falk, B. 2000. *The heart of the matter: Using standards and assessment to learn.* Portsmouth, NH: Heinemann.

Gartrell, D. 2004. *The power of guidance: Teaching social-emotional skills in early childhood classrooms*. Clifton Park, NY: Thomson Delmar Learning; Washington, DC: NAEYC.

Gestwicki, C. 1999. *Developmentally appropriate practice, curriculum, and development in early education*. Clifton Park, NY: Thomson Delmar Learning.

[Head Start] *Program performance standards for the operation of Head Start programs by grantee and delegate agencies* (45-CFS 1304). Available online: www.access.gpo.gov/nara/cfr/waisidx_04/45cfr1304_04.html. These regulations include *Facilities, materials, and equipment* (45-CFS 1304.53). [For latest updates: www.headstartinfo.org/publications/perf_stds/update.htm.]

Head Start Bureau. 2003, Summer. *The Head Start path to positive child outcomes*. Washington, DC: U.S. Department of Health and Human Services, Administration on Children, Youth, and Families. Available online: www.headstartinfo.org/pdf/hsoutcomespath28ppREV.pdf. [The Head Start Information and Publication Center at www.headstartinfo.org also offers resources on curriculum, education/teaching strategies, and other materials to serve Head Start and other children from low-income populations.]

Healy, L. 2001. Applying theory to practice: Using developmentally appropriate strategies to help children draw. *Young Children* 56 (3): 28–30.

Helm, J.H., & L. Katz. 2001. *Young investigators: The project approach in the early years*. New York: Teachers College Press. Available from NAEYC.

Heroman, C., & C. Jones. 2004. *Literacy: The Creative Curriculum approach*. Washington, DC: Teaching Strategies.

Hirsch, E. 1996. *The block book*. 3d ed. Washington DC: NAEYC.

Hohmann, M. 2002. *Fee, fie, phonemic awareness: 130 prereading activities for preschoolers*. Ypsilanti, MI: High/Scope Press.

Hohmann, M., & D.P. Weikart. 2002. *Educating young children: Active learning practices for preschool and child care programs*. 2d ed. Ypsilanti, MI: High/Scope Press.

Hyson, M. 2000. Professional Development. "Is it OK to have calendar time?" Look up to the star . . . Look within yourself! *Young Children* 55 (6): 60–61.

IRA (International Reading Association) & NAEYC. 1998. *Learning to read and write: Developmentally appropriate practices for young children*. Joint Position Statement. Washington, DC: NAEYC. Also available online: www.naeyc.org/about/positions/pdf/PSREAD98.pdf. Also in Neuman, Copple, & Bredekamp 2000.

Jablon, J.R., A.L. Dombro, & M.O. Dichtelmiller. 1999. *The power of observation.* Washington, DC: Teaching Strategies.

Jalongo, M.R. 2004. *Young children and picture books.* 2d ed. Washington, DC: NAEYC.

Kaiser, B., & J.S. Rasminsky. 1999. *Meeting the challenge: Effective strategies for challenging behaviors in early childhood environments.* Ottawa, ONT: Canadian Child Care Federation.

Koralek, D.G., series ed. *Spotlight on young children.* Washington, DC: NAEYC. [Series titles on language, math, science, play, assessment, and the creative arts.]

Koralek, D.G., ed. 2005. Developmentally appropriate practice in 2005: Updates from the field. Special issue. *Young Children* 60 (4).

Koralek, D.G., L.J. Colker, & D.T. Dodge. 1995. *The what, why, and how of high-quality early childhood education: A guide for on-site supervision.* Rev. ed. Washington, DC: NAEYC.

Koralek, D.G., D.T. Dodge, & P. Pizzolongo. 2004. *Caring for preschool children.* 3d ed. Washington, DC: Teaching Strategies.

Landry, S.H. 2005. *Effective early childhood programs: Turning knowledge into action.* Houston, TX: University of Texas, Health Science Center.

McAfee, O., D.J. Leong, & E. Bodrova. 2004. *Basics of assessment: A primer for early childhood educators.* Washington, DC: NAEYC.

Meier, D.R. 2004. *The young child's memory for words: Developing first and second language and literacy.* New York: Teachers College Press.

NAEYC. 1996. Developmentally appropriate practice in early childhood programs serving children from birth through age 8. Position Statement. Washington, DC: Author. Also available online: www.naeyc.org/about/positions/pdf/PSDAP98.pdf.

NAEYC. 2005, April. NAEYC code of ethical conduct. Position Statement. Washington, DC: Author. Also available online: www.naeyc.org/about/positions/PSETH05.asp.

NAEYC. 2005. *Self-study kit for program quality improvement.* Washington, DC: Author. [Available from the NAEYC Academy for Early Childhood Program Accreditation: www.naeyc.org/accreditation/academy.asp.]

National Resource Center for Health and Safety in Child Care. 2002. *Caring for our children: National Health and Safety Performance Standards: Guidelines for out-of-home child care programs.* 2d ed. Department of Health and Human Services, Health Resources and Services Administration, Maternal and Child Health Bureau. Available online: http://nrc.uchsc.edu/CFOC/. [Database of states' licensing requirements also available: http://nrc.uchsc.edu/STATES/states.htm.]

National Resource Center for Health and Safety in Child Care. 2002. *Stepping stones to using Caring for Our Children.* Department of Health and Human Services, Health Resources and Services Administration, Maternal and Child Health Bureau. Available online: http://nrc.uchsc.edu/STEPPING/SteppingStones.pdf. [Database of states' licensing requirements also available: http://nrc.uchsc.edu/STATES/states.htm.]

Neuman, S.B., C. Copple, & S. Bredekamp. 2000. *Learning to read and write: Developmentally appropriate practices for young children.* Washington, DC: NAEYC.

Owocki, G. 2001. *Make way for literacy: Teaching the way young children learn.* Portsmouth, NH: Heinemann; Washington, DC: NAEYC.

Routman, R. 2003. *Reading essentials: The specifics you need to teach reading well.* Portsmouth, NH: Heinemann.

Rushton, S.P. 2001. Applying brain research to create developmentally appropriate learning environments. *Young Children* 56 (5): 76–82.

Sandall, S., M.E. McLean, & B.J. Smith. 2000. *DEC recommended practices in early intervention/early childhood special education.* Denver, CO: Division for Early Childhood (DEC) of the Council for Exceptional Children (CEC).

Sandall, S.R., & I.S. Schwartz. 2002. *Building blocks for teaching preschoolers with special needs.* Baltimore, MD: Paul H. Brookes. Distributed by Redleaf Press.

Sanders, S. 2002. *Active for life: Developmentally appropriate movement programs for young children.* Washington, DC: NAEYC.

Schickedanz, J. 1999. *Much more than the ABCs: The early stages of reading and writing.* Washington, DC: NAEYC.

Schweinhart, L.J., & D.P. Weikart. 1997. The High/Scope preschool curriculum comparison study through age 23. *Early Childhood Research Quarterly* 12 (2).

Shonkoff, J.P., & D.A. Phillips, eds. 2000. *From neurons to neighborhoods: The science of early childhood development.* Washington, DC: National Academies Press. Available online: www.nap.edu.

Tabors, P. 1997. *One child, two languages: A guide for preschool educators of children learning English as a second language.* Baltimore, MD: Paul H. Brookes.

Tarr, P. 2001. *Early childhood classrooms: What art educators can learn from Reggio Emilia.* Reston, VA: National Art Education Association.

Torbert, M., & L. Schneider. [1993] 2005. *Follow me too: A handbook of movement activities for three- to five-year-olds.* Washington, DC: NAEYC.

Vogel, N. 1999. *Getting started: Materials and equipment for active learning preschools.* Ypsilanti, MI: High/Scope Press.

Wardle, F. 1999. In praise of developmentally appropriate practice. *Young Children* 54 (6): 4–11.

Weitzman, E., & J. Greenberg. 2002. *Learning language and loving it: A guide to promoting children's social and language development in early childhood settings.* Toronto: Hanen Centre.

Worth, K., & S. Grollman. 2003. *Worms, shadows, and whirlpools: Science in the early childhood classroom.* Portsmouth, NH: Heinemann; Washington, DC: NAEYC.

Zigler, E., D. Singer, & S. Bishop-Josef. 2004. *Children's play: The roots of reading.* Washington, DC: Zero to Three.

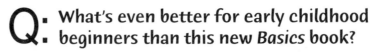

Q: What's even better for early childhood beginners than this new *Basics* book?

A: This book WITH video resources that bring best practice to life! . . .

Looking at the Basics of Developmentally Appropriate Practice

A great fit with the new *Basics* book and versatile enough to be shown as part of any beginner-level discussion of DAP. Some instructors and trainers will want to show it when learners are using *Developmentally Appropriate Practice in Early Childhood Programs* or other texts. Children ages 3 to 6 are the focus. Produced by RISE Learning Solutions, in collaboration with NAEYC. Approximately 30 min. **VHS #860 / DVD #861**

Tools for Teaching Developmentally Appropriate Practice

With powerful images and clear language, these videos communicate the key concepts of good early childhood practice, showcasing excellent teaching in a wide range of programs, including infant/toddler rooms, child care centers, preschools, family child care homes, kindergartens, and primary-grade classrooms. Widely used in courses, staff development sessions, and other training sessions, 180+ minutes of video offer participants a deeper understanding of the core content of the early childhood knowledge base; effective and easy ways to organize DAP content to teach it to other people; and new tools and strategies to communicate complex concepts to varied audiences. Produced by RISE Learning Solutions, in collaboration with NAEYC. **VHS, 4-video set #800**

. . . and the classic, comprehensive exploration of DAP.

Developmentally Appropriate Practice in Early Childhood Programs—Revised Edition.

This comprehensive volume spells out the principles underlying developmentally appropriate practice and guidelines for classroom decision making, including the importance of the social and cultural context in considering best practice. For all engaged in the care and education of infants and toddlers, preschoolers, or primary-grade children, this book offers an overview of each period of development and extensive examples of practices appropriate and inappropriate with children in that age group. #234

Early years are learning years

Become a member of NAEYC, and help make them count!

Just as you help young children learn and grow, the National Association for the Education of Young Children—your professional organization—supports you in the work you love. NAEYC is the world's largest early childhood education organization, with a national network of local, state, and regional Affiliates. We are nearly 100,000 members working together to bring high-quality early learning opportunities to all children from birth through age eight.

Since 1926, NAEYC has provided educational services and resources for people working with children, including:

• *Young Children*, the award-winning journal (six issues a year) for early childhood educators

• **Books, posters, brochures, and videos** to support your work with young children and families

• **The NAEYC Annual Conference**, which brings tens of thousands of people together from across the country and around the world to share their expertise and ideas on the education of young children

• **Insurance plans** for members and programs

• **A voluntary accreditation system** to help programs reach national standards for high-quality early childhood education

• **Global Alliance for the Education of Young Children** to foster cross-national exchanges with organizations that share NAEYC's commitment to young children and excellence in early childhood education.

• **www.naeyc.org**—a dynamic Web site with up-to-date information on all of our services and resources

To join NAEYC

To find a complete list of membership benefits and options or to join NAEYC online, visit **www.naeyc.org/membership.** Or you can mail this form to us.

(Membership must be for an individual, not a center or school.)

Name _____

Address _____

City_____ State_____ ZIP_____

E-mail_____

Phone (H)_____ (W)_____

❏ New member ❏ Renewal ID # _____

Affiliate name/number _____

To determine your dues, you must visit **www.naeyc.org/membership** or call 800-424-2460, ext. 2002.

Indicate your payment option

❏ VISA ❏ MasterCard ❏ AmEx ❏ Discover

Card #_____

Exp. date _____

Cardholder's name _____

Signature _____

Note: By joining NAEYC you also become a member of your state and local Affiliates.

Send this form and payment to

NAEYC, PO Box 97156, Washington, DC 20090-7156